English for International Business

English for international business : fun in the sun ;
Linda Wenzek-Barth, Margaret Ann Doty.
Offenbach, Jünger Verlag 1995
ISBN 3-89467-310-9

© 1995 Jünger Verlag, Offenbach . Frankfurt
Lizenzausgabe: PLS Lernsysteme, Solothurn

Verlagsinformation:
Jünger Service, Schumannstrasse 161, 63069 Offenbach
Tel: 069/840003-22 (-0) Fax: 069/840003-33

Alle Rechte vorbehalten. Nachdruck, auch auszugsweise, jede Art der Vervielfältigung
sowie Verwendung in Seminaren ausschließlich mit schriftlicher Genehmigung des
Verlags. Printed in Germany.

English for International Business

Fun in the Sun

Kommunikatives Wirtschaftsenglisch

Businesspark • Zettachring 8 • 70567 Stuttgart
Tel.: 0711 / 728-7331 • Fax: 0711 - 728-6533
E-Mail: 101620.2276@compuserve.com

Offenbach · Frankfurt

Autorinnen:
LINDA WENZEK-BARTH, Deutsch-Amerikanerin, Bachelor´s Degree in Journalistik und Germanistik der Colorado State University. Langjährige Erfahrung in Akquisition und Marketing. Suggestopädin und selbständige Trainerin.
MARGARET ANN DOTY, Amerikanerin, Bachelor´s Degree in General Business und Englisch, New York Regents University. Langjährige administrative Erfahrung in internationalen Firmen. Suggestopädin und selbständige Trainerin.

Fachliche Beratung:
HELMUT J. KRIETE, Dipl. Betriebswirt und Schiffahrtskaufmann, Leiter der Abteilung Fremdsprachen an der Wirtschafts- und Sozialakademie.
MICHAEL LAWLOR, Gründer und Direktor des Western Language Centre Ltd., Kemble, Gloucestershire, England. Langjährige Erfahrung im Export-Management. Mitglied des British Institute of Management. Autor fachspezifischer Bücher.
DR. REINGARD MULTER, MA Deutsch und Philosophie, Promotion an der University of California, L.A. Dozentin für Deutsch an Universitäten in USA und Italien sowie an öffentlichen Bildungsinstituten.

Übersetzung:
DR. REINGARD MULTER, Bremerhaven
BRIGITTE SCHWITALLA, Dipl. Übersetzerin, suggestopädische Firmentrainings im Bereich Sprachen, Weiterbildung, Institutsleiterin von SINIT, Köln.
CORNELIA ZARTH, Trainerin in der betrieblichen Fortbildung (Englisch, Französisch, Kommunikation, Suggestopädie), Düsseldorf.

Unser besonderer Dank gilt:
MANFRED BARTH, Jurist im Personalwesen.
MOYA IRVINE, BA (Honours) in Deutsch der Bristol University, Redakteurin, Übersetzerin.
ECON VERLAG, für die freundliche Genehmigung der auszugsweisen Wiedergabe und Übersetzung der 'Eigentore: weltweit' aus: Commer, Heinz "Der neue Manager-Knigge", Düsseldorf, 1993

Illustrationen: Franziska Seifert, Hamburg
Layout/Cartoons: Roland Bühs, Bremen
Tonproduktion: M. Dyke Studios, Bremen
Druck: rgg Druck- und Verlagshaus, Braunschweig

TABLE OF CONTENTS

Introduction	Page 7
How to use this program	Page 9
Contents of the CDs/Cassettes	Page 11
Texts of Mental Relaxations	Page 12

Corporate Strategy/Meeting People

Unit 1 — Page 16
James Thorne attends the corporate strategy meeting of the Sun Club division of *Sun International*. A new project is discussed and the European sales directors are requested to talk about strategic objectives within their fields of expertise.

Skills 1 — Page 83
- nationalities review
- greetings/picking up a colleague at the airport
- minutes of a meeting
- a business lunch and chit chat
- socializing at a party

Negotiations

Unit 2 — Page 24
William Garfield, a potential joint venture partner, arrives from the Virgin Islands for negotiations. The objective of this meeting with Jonathan Wadsworth, James Thorne and Penny McCloud will be to put down any agreements they come to in a letter of intent.

Skills 2 — Page 94
- familiarize yourself with golf
- useful phrases for business meetings
- phrasal verb "to look"
- crossword puzzle of business terms
- cultural awareness

Factors to be considered/Travel arrangements

Unit 3 — Page 32
Penny McCloud reports on her research for the feasibility study. Factors to be considered include environment, economic and social policies. Afterwards she makes travel arrangements and reschedules appointments for James Thorne.

Skills 3 — Page 103
- writing effective faxes
- making travel arrangements
- checking in at the airport
- using prepositions
- solving a puzzle of time
- similar pairs of words
- phrasal verb "to put"

Money matters

Unit 4 — Page 40
James Thorne meets with José Aquilar in Madrid to discuss some financial matters regarding the Virgin Islands project. Afterwards, James Thorne goes to a bank to cash a traveller´s check.

Skills 4 — Page 113
- building and using word pairs
- finding your way around a balance sheet
- transactions at a bank
- telex and E-mail abbreviations
- phrasal verb "to take"

TABLE OF CONTENTS

Human Resources

Unit 5	Page 49	Skills 5	Page 125

Upon his arrival in Frankfurt, James Thorne rents a car and then joins Fritz Fischer in interviewing a promising candidate, Otto Huber, for the position of club manager in the Virgin Islands.

- writing a CV and cover letter
- hiring a car
- what is TQM?
- an organizational chart
- phrasal verb "to call"

Marketing and Advertising

Unit 6	Page 57	Skills 6	Page 136

In Rome, James Thorne meets with Adriana Saladino to discuss the marketing strategy for the new club and the ad agency to be used for the ad campaign. Afterwards they have an appointment with the representative of an ad agency.

- marketing a product
- describing trends
- analyzing charts
- spelling
- pronunciation of similar words
- phrasal verb "to go"

PR and Presentations

Unit 7	Page 65	Skills 7	Page 143

Penny McCloud joins James Thorne on a trip to Paris in order to visit a travel trade fair and to attend Pierre Duclot's presentation on the club´s new facilities. But not everything goes as planned and this time Penny McCloud comes to the rescue.

- using visual aids
- useful expressions for a presentation
- phrasal verb "to make"
- introducing a guest speaker
- congratulatory speeches
- using similar words correctly
- opposites

Handling Complaints/Communication

Unit 8	Page 73	Skills 8	Page 151

During his meeting with Jannie van Vliet in Amsterdam, James Thorne explains how to handle complaints and clears up some problems involving false advertising. Meanwhile, a major change is about to take place at the Virgin Islands...

- receiving messages on an answering machine
- telephoning
- handling complaints
- crossword of telephone phrases
- letter of apology
- phrasal verb "to keep"

Answer key	Page 161
Transcript	Page 166
Grammar Reference	Page 178
Appendix: American and British English	Page 191
International Airline Alphabet/British Telecom	Page 195
Telex Abbreviations	Page 196
International Etiquette	Page 198
Faux pas Worldwide	Page 199
Do´s in Great Britain and the United States	Page 203

INTRODUCTION

Um den steigenden Anforderungen am Arbeitsplatz und im internationalen Markt gerecht zu werden, vermittelt **English for International Business** in kompakter Form über 1 200 der wichtigsten Vokabeln und Redewendungen für den Bereich Wirtschaftsamerikanisch/Wirtschaftsenglisch. Darüber hinaus liefert es aktuelles Know-how und zahlreiche Tips und Fertigkeiten aus vielen Bereichen der internationalen Geschäftswelt. Neueste Management-Trends und Erfolgsstrategien werden interessant dargestellt und wichtige Sprachstrukturen lebendig vermittelt.

Ihr Kenntnisstand nach Absolvieren dieses Kurses entspricht in etwa dem des **London Chamber of Commerce and Industry** (English for Business, Level 2). Ihre Voraussetzungen für diesen Kurs sollten – neben Neugier und Interesse an Ihrer persönlichen Weiterbildung – gute allgemeine Englischkenntnisse sein.

Neben neuestem Faktenwissen und moderner Wirtschaftssprache spielte bei der Konzeption dieses Programms ein weiterer wesentlicher Faktor eine Rolle: die **Superlearning-Methode**. Superlearning (oder auch Suggestopädie) ist eine ganzheitliche Lehr- und Lernmethode, die sowohl Körper als auch Geist anspricht. Sie wurde in den 60er Jahren von Dr. Georgi Lozanov entwickelt, dessen Ziel es war, neue Lernmethoden und Lernstrategien zu finden, die ein leichteres und zugleich angenehmeres Lernen ermöglichen. Er entdeckte, daß das Zusammenwirken von mentaler Entspannung, klassischer Musik, rhythmischer Sprechweise und positiv motivierenden Suggestionen den Lernprozeß um ein Vielfaches beschleunigen kann. Anfang der 80er Jahre wurde die Suggestopädie auch in Deutschland bekannt und wird seitdem vor allem im Bereich des Fremdsprachenunterrichts kontinuierlich weiterentwickelt.

Die wichtigsten Elemente des Superlearning sind:

- entspannte und angenehme Lernatmosphäre
- spannender Lernroman, mit klassischer Musik unterlegt
- Übungen, die Spaß machen und die Kreativität anregen
- ganzheitliches Lernen

Das Ergebnis: Mit Superlearning lernen Sie erheblich streßfreier, effektiver und schneller als mit herkömmlichen Lernmethoden.

Entspanntes Lernen ist ein ganz wesentlicher Aspekt des Superlearning. Durch gezielte Entspannung wird unser Gehirn in den sogenannten „Alpha-Zustand" versetzt, in dem wir entspannt und zugleich hochgradig konzentriert und wach sind. Im Alpha-Zustand ist unser Gehirn wesentlich aufnahmefähiger, und wir können mehr Lernstoff verarbeiten. Aus diesem Grund finden Sie auf den Tonträgern mentale Entspannungstrainings. Durch einfaches Zuhören erreichen Sie in kurzer Zeit den Alpha-Zustand. Diese Fähigkeit sowie die Musikunterlegung der Lernkonzerte ermöglichen ein entspanntes und angenehmes Lernen und garantieren eine hohe Behaltensleistung.

INTRODUCTION

Was man gelernt hat, das „sitzt", denn der Stoff wird beim Superlearning durch mehrere Lernkanäle aufgenommen, wie durch die Augen, durch die Ohren, durch Bewegung etc., und wird dadurch auf vielfälige Weise im Gehirn verankert. Zusätzlich gewährleistet die interessante Geschichte, die in Form eines Romans geschrieben ist, einen emotionalen Zugang zum Lehrtext und spricht eine Vielzahl von Sinneskanälen an. Durch diese Art des Lernens wird nicht nur die linke, analytische, sondern auch die rechte, kreative Gehirnhälfte angesprochen und die Kapazitäten des Gehirns werden optimal genutzt.

Der **Lernroman** zeichnet sich dadurch aus, daß in ihm mehr Lernstoff angeboten wird, als der Lerner bewußt bewältigen kann. Dieses Prinzip des „vergrößerten Inputs" beruht vereinfacht gesagt darauf, daß, wo mehr „gesät" wird, auch mehr „geerntet" werden kann. Auch unbewußt aufgenommene Informationen werden in unserem Gedächtnis gespeichert und können unter bestimmten Bedingungen aktiviert werden.

Der **Übungsteil** vertieft und übt die Strukturen und Anforderungen aus dem Textteil. Systematisch werden hier die Fähigkeiten, sich schriftlich und mündlich auszudrücken, wichtige Informationen aus Schriftstücken zu entnehmen und englische Gespräche zu verfolgen, entwickelt und verbessert. Darüber hinaus vertieft der Übungsteil Faktenwissen bezüglich aktueller Management-Trends sowie klassischer Standards aus dem Geschäftsbereich.

Wir wünschen Ihnen viel Spaß und viel Erfolg mit diesem Kurs!

HOW TO USE THIS PROGRAM

Bitte lesen Sie diese Lernanleitung aufmerksam durch, bevor Sie mit dem Kurs beginnen. Nur wenn Sie den grundlegenden Aufbau dieses Kurses verstehen, werden Sie effektiv damit lernen können und die von Ihnen gewünschten Erfolge schnell erzielen.

Vorbereitungen

1. Die Lernumgebung

Die Umgebung, in der man lernt, beeinflußt die Lernergebnisse. Machen Sie sich deshalb vor Beginn des Kurses einige Gedanken darüber, ob Sie Ihre Lernumgebung als angenehm empfinden. Das Zimmer sollte ruhig und gut beleuchtet, die Temperatur angenehm und Ihre Sitzgelegenheit bequem sein (am besten eignen sich Sessel mit hoher Rückenlehne, an die man den Kopf auflegen kann).
Außerdem sollte Ihnen ein CD-Player bzw. Cassettenrecorder oder Diskman®/Walkman® in guter Qualität zur Verfügung stehen.

2. Das Entspannungstraining

Die Entspannung spielt bei der Superlearning-Methode eine wesentliche Rolle. Denn im Zustand tiefer Entspannung ist unser Gehirn besonders aufnahmefähig. Nutzen Sie deshalb die Entspannungselemente auf den Tonträgern. Schon nach kurzer Zeit erreichen Sie den sogenannten „Alpha-Zustand", in dem Sie sich den neuen Lernstoff besonders leicht einprägen können. Der „Alpha-Zustand" kündigt sich durch ein leichtes, sehr angenehmes Wärme- und Schweregefühl in den Armen und Beinen an.
Manchen - besonders streßgeplagten - Menschen könnte es anfangs schwerfallen, sich in einen Entspannungszustand zu versetzen. Beginnen Sie trotzdem mit dem Sprachkurs. Ihre Fähigkeit, sich zu entspannen, wird sich im Laufe des Kurses in jedem Fall verbessern.

Lernschritte

1. Das aktive Lernkonzert

Während Sie sich das aktive Lernkonzert der jeweiligen Unit auf der CD/Cassette anhören, lesen Sie bitte den Lernroman im Buch leise mit. Schauen Sie sich dabei ruhig die Übersetzung an, damit Sie wissen, was auf englisch gelesen wird. Hören Sie sich bitte erst den gesamten Text der Unit an, bevor Sie etwas nachschlagen. Die recht langsame, aber betonte Vortragsweise des englischen Sprechers, unterlegt mit dynamischer klassischer Musik, erleichtert das Einfühlen in den Klang der englischen Sprache. Sie nehmen unbewußt viele wichtige Informationen über das Vokabular und den Aufbau der englischen Sprache auf. Beim zweiten Anhören empfehlen wir Ihnen, die einzelnen Textsequenzen in den Pausen laut mitzusprechen.

HOW TO USE THIS PROGRAM

2. Das passive Lernkonzert
Nach dem aktiven Lernkonzert führen Sie bitte noch nicht die Übungen durch, sondern hören Sie sich das passive Lernkonzert an. Legen Sie dazu Ihr Buch beiseite. Eingeführt durch die mentale Entspannung (Text siehe Seite 12 bis 15, ohne Übersetzung) hören Sie den kompletten Text der Unit hier noch einmal unterlegt mit moderner Entspannungsmusik. Während der Text im aktiven Lernkonzert von einem britischen Sprecher gelesen wird, haben wir für diese zweite Präsentation des Gesamttextes eine amerikanische Sprecherin gewählt, um Ihnen auch das amerikanische Englisch akustisch nicht vorzuenthalten.
Nach der Präsentation der beiden Lernkonzerte fühlen Sie sich vielleicht etwas müde. Darum sollten Sie an dieser Stelle eine kleine Pause machen, sich bewegen, das Fenster öffnen und sich strecken.
Hinweis: Sollten Sie während des passiven Lernkonzertes einschlafen, holen Sie diese Lernphase nach, wenn Sie wieder ausgeruht sind. Die passiven Lernkonzerte eignen sich übrigens nicht zum Anhören während des Autofahrens!

3. Die Aktivierung
Nachdem Sie den Text der Unit nun zweimal gehört haben, können Sie jetzt mit dem Übungsteil (Skills) beginnen. Die schriftlichen Übungen befinden sich im Buch. Auf den CDs/Cassetten finden Sie zusätzliche Übungen, die das Hörverständnis bzw. die Sprechfertigkeit trainieren. Wir empfehlen Ihnen, die entsprechenden Übungen mehrmals durchzuführen. Überprüfen Sie bitte nach jeder Übung die Ergebnisse anhand der Lösungen im Buch (Answer key).

4. Die Triaden
Eingeführt durch eine Kurzentspannung werden in den Triaden die zentralen Vokabeln und Redewendungen der Lektion im Dreiertakt (englisch - deutsch - englisch) erneut vorgetragen. Sie haben mehrere Möglichkeiten, die Triaden zu nutzen.
Sie können sie aktiv nutzen, indem Sie den englischen Text in der dafür vorgesehenen Pause nachsprechen oder übersetzen. Auf diese Weise schulen Sie Ihr Hörverständnis, Ihre Aussprache und können überprüfen, wieviel Sie bereits verstehen.
Sie können die Triaden aber auch passiv nutzen, indem Sie die Texte ganz entspannt verfolgen. Lassen Sie die Geschichte als inneren Film im Geist an sich vorüberziehen, denn so prägen sich die Wörter leichter ein.

Wir empfehlen Ihnen, alle Text- und Übungsteile mehrmals anzuhören.

Enjoy yourself - viel Spaß!

11 CONTENTS OF THE CD´S/CASSETTES

CD Entspannungstraining

Die 8 CDs/Cassetten enthalten jeweils die kompletten Texte einer Unit und sind wie folgt aufgebaut:

CD/Cassette Seite A
1. Aktives Lernkonzert (ca. 15 Minuten)
2. Entspannung (ca. 5 Minuten)
3. Passives Lernkonzert (ca. 17 Minuten)
4. Stretching (ca. 0,5 Minuten)

CD/Cassette Seite B
5. Übungen (zwischen 2 und 6 Minuten je nach Lektion)
6. Kurzentspannung (ca. 0,5 Minuten)
7. Triaden (ca. 25 Minuten)
8. Stretching (ca. 1 Minute)

Sprecher:
Linda Wenzek-Barth, Jack Brigden, Christin Pols, Clive Gray

RELAXATION 12

Eagle Meditation

It's time to feel good now and to relax. You find a comfortable position for your body. Close your eyes and listen to the soothing sound of the music and breathe calmly, slowly and deeply.

Now you are an eagle, sitting on your favorite branch in your favorite tree, high up in the Rocky Mountains of Colorado.

As you sit here and look down into the valley, you slowly spread your wings, feel a nice cool breeze blowing through your feathers and slowly lift off the branch and begin to fly circling higher and higher, slowly around, as the air carries you gently through the clear blue sky.

You breathe in deeply the crisp clean air and gradually circle down, down to the evergreen trees below and here, gliding over the tops of the trees below, you begin to hear a sound in the distance.

And gradually you see a blue ribbon of water, winding its way through the woods, and you circle and begin to follow the river upstream.

And slowly the rushing sound of water becomes louder and louder until you see a magnificent waterfall cascading down a mountain into a pool of water.

And as you fly closer, you see all the colors of a rainbow in the mist that's rising from the water below. The colors are almost fluorescent and as you fly by, you can feel the fresh spray of water and it feels refreshing and good.

And as you slowly circle around, you start to fly back in the direction of your favorite tree and you arrive and land on your favorite branch.

You feel safe and secure here, at peace and in harmony with everything around you.

RELAXATION

The sea

Make yourself comfortable and let the earth and the music carry you as you relax and take a moment to concentrate on your breathing. Slowly, deeply, in and out, like the waves of an ocean.
With each breath you feel your body relaxing and your thoughts start wandering to the sounds in the distance, the sound of waves drawing you forward as you´re walking through the sand dunes, around tufts of grass, gently blowing in the wind. As you walk, with each step, your feet sink into the sand, warm and soft between your toes and around your feet, as the sound of waves gradually becomes louder, until there, over the last sanddune, you see the dark blue water spreading out as far as the eye can see, the sunlight dancing on the waves, as you come closer to the water.
And here the sand becomes cool and moist, and as you stand at the edge of the water, the tip of a wave washes tenderly over your feet and gently moves out again into the sea.
And as the breeze blows softly through your hair, you lift your face to the warmth of the sun and take a deep breath of fresh sea air, almost tasting the salt on the tip of your tongue and as you breathe deeply, you feel at peace and in harmony with yourself and everything around you, calm and quiet, you enjoy the blue light.

RELAXATION

The meadow

Close your eyes and lean comfortably into your chair. Listen to the soothing sound of the music and breathe calmly in and out. It´s a warm wonderful summer day. You´re walking through a lush, green meadow decorated with colorful wildflowers.
You breathe in deeply the fresh clean air and at the same time you can smell the grass and the beautiful flowers all around you.
It´s peaceful and still here. You only hear the buzzing sound of insects nearby and off in the distance, you can hear birds singing.
A light breeze is blowing across the meadow and as you watch the long blades of grass sway in the wind like waves on an ocean back and forth and to and fro and as you walk, your steps are feather-light and you feel the soft cushion of grass like a carpet under your feet.
With each step you feel lighter and lighter and more and more in harmony with the natural beauty around you.
You find a nice soft spot to lay down and relax. Gazing at the bright blue sky above, you begin to stretch out your arms and your legs and you close your eyes and enjoy the warmth of the sun soaking into the skin on your arms, on your legs and on your face.
As you listen to the sounds of the birds singing, you feel the breeze gently blowing through the grass and you feel at peace and in harmony with everything around you.
You´re happy just to be here, peaceful, calm and quiet.

15 RELAXATION

The Scottish highlands

You are walking through the rugged Scottish highlands. The air is clear and cool. Your legs feel strong as you stride effortlessly along. There are wild, rounded hills, rocky and covered with purple heather. The ground is stony, but you are wearing strong boots. Up you go, along the path through the heather. Past ancient rocks like strong old giants, their skin - yellow, orange, purple. Here and there a huge old tree stretches up. You smell the fresh clean air ...
You hear the sound of the gentle wind and bees buzzing in the heather. You smile to yourself and a wonderful feeling of freedom wells up in you, freedom and strength.
You've reached the top of the hill now, and you look down at the loch in the valley below. It looks still and mysterious, greyish blue, its surface covered with countless ripples.
But here the wind is stronger, and a mist is starting to blow down from the mountains nearby. It is time to go back. You head off towards the little cottage where you're staying. It's a small grey stone house with a stone fence around it. You open the door, take off your boots, hang up your jacket, and go over to the comfortable armchair by the fireplace. How good it is to feel the warmth of the fire! You can hear it crackle as new twigs start to burn. You sink into the soft warm chair and relax, completely contented.

Returning

Slowly, in your own tempo, come back to this room and feel the energy flowing into your fingers and toes.
And stretch your arms and legs, take a few deep breaths, open your eyes and once again, be totally here.

1

It is a cool, clear morning in the south of London. The smell of autumn is in the air, mixed with a fresh breeze coming from the Thames. A stylishly-dressed, good-looking man in his late thirties whistles a popular tune as he crosses the street and enters a tall building made of glass.

Taking the lift up to the tenth floor, he briefly looks at his reflection in the mirrors lining the walls. Quickly running his fingers through his wavy dark hair, he steps out of the lift and is happy to see his assistant, Penny McCloud. A pretty, 35-year-old woman with flaming-red hair, Penny looks professional, yet feminine in her slim-waisted blue suit. She is sitting on a sofa next to a cheerful-looking woman in her forties. They are having a very lively discussion and James can detect an Italian accent as he approaches them.

James:
Good morning ladies. Isn't it a lovely day today?

Penny: (surprised)
Oh James, I didn't see you come in. I'd like you to meet our new sales director for the Rome office, Ms. Adriana Saladino. Ms. Saladino, may I introduce...

James steps forward with a friendly smile and reaches out his hand.

James:
Thorne, James Thorne. I'm very pleased to meet you Ms. Saladino.

Adriana:
How do you do, Mr. Thorne? I've heard a lot about you.

James:
Oh? Only good things I hope. But please, call me James.

Penny:
James likes to be on a first name basis with everyone in the company. Although he has a British father, his mother is an American and many of their habits have rubbed off on him.

Adriana:
Hmm, I think that's nice. I can imagine the atmosphere is less formal in the office that way.

James: (smiling)
Penny doesn't approve of all of my habits though. I'm addicted to chocolate, for example. Thanks to Penny, I've switched to eating chocolate-covered raisins. At least I get some vitamins with my chocolate that way.

Adriana: (laughing)
Oh, that's funny! I doubt it's a very healthy way to get your daily dose of vitamins though.

James:
I'm sure Penny would agree with you. She's very health-conscious. But I'd be lost without her. The meeting hasn't started yet has it Penny?

Penny: (glancing at her watch)
No, but it should be starting any minute now.
Our Senior Vice President, Jonathan Wadsworth and the other European sales directors are already waiting.

The three of them enter the large, wood-panelled conference room. A group of five people are already seated around a beautiful, oval-shaped mahogany table. As James and the two women walk across the lush, light-blue carpet, Adriana notices pictures of holiday destinations decorating the walls.
The Senior Executive Vice President of the Sun Club division of Sun International is sitting at the head of the table. His silvery-grey hair contrasts nicely with his black suit and red tie. Energetic by nature, he seems younger than his age of 62. As he sees the group entering, he quickly rises to greet them.

Jonathan:
James, Penny, it's good to see you. Ms. Saladino, I'm glad you could join us. Please take a seat. Penny will be taking the minutes of the meeting. Let's begin now, shall we?
As you all know, I've asked you here today to discuss our Virgin Islands project. In addition to your duties as sales directors of our European branch offices, each of you has an area of expertise that will be beneficial to the success of our project.
The Sun Club division of Sun International would like to build a new club resort on the Virgin Islands. This is the first time we will offer conference facilities in one of our clubs and it will require a whole new marketing strategy. Most of you already know our trouble-shooter, James Thorne.

Adriana: (looking confused)
Excuse me Mr. Wadsworth, but I'm not familiar with the expression "trouble-shooter". Could someone explain it to me, please?

Jannie Van Vliet (Dutch Sales Director):
I think I can help. A trouble-shooter goes where the trouble is. He's our man in a time of crisis and often acts as a mediator when problems arise.

Jonathan:
That's correct Ms. Van Vliet. Mr. Thorne has been with the company for over 15 years now and his international background has helped us solve cross-cultural problems numerous times.

James: (looking at Adriana)
Thanks to my father, who was a diplomat, I had the opportunity to live in and experience the cultures of many different countries. That's made it a lot easier for me to avoid problems due to simple misunderstandings.

Jonathan:
Precisely, and that's why we feel James is our man to supervise the Virgin Islands project. We want to foresee trouble before it arises.

Pierre Duclot (French Sales Director):
Do you anticipate any particular problems connected with this project?

James:
What I think Mr. Wadsworth is concerned about are the factors, both internal and external, that need to be taken into consideration.
Firstly, we have no experience in marketing conference facilities and secondly, we have little knowledge about the Virgin Islands and what building a resort there will involve.

Jonathan:
You've hit the nail on the head, James. And that's the first item on our agenda today, a discussion about our corporate strategy for this project.
In preparation for this meeting, each of you was asked to think about strategic objectives within your field. Let's do some brainstorming now and try to incorporate your ideas into our overall strategy.
Mr. Fischer, as our hotel management expert, why don't you begin?

Mr. Fritz Fischer (German Sales Director):
Well, I always feel we must identify our greatest strengths and make use of them. We should be goal-oriented in cultivating those strengths and then combine them with new services like the conference facilities we're now planning. The big question is, what do we offer that our competitors don't?
Being unique will be the key to our success!

Jannie: (nodding her head)
I agree. Being innovative is definitely important. As an entertainment expert, I've discovered that our level of performance has to be improved constantly. I think this pertains to our corporate strategy as well. It's important to collect all of our creative ideas and systematically evaluate them. Standing still would be a step backwards.

Pierre Duclot:
And we should by all means look at what our competitors are doing. There's no sense in wasting time working on some problem others have already solved. We ought to make use of their knowledge and experience.

James:
You're right. As a matter of fact, I would take that a step further. I believe we should cooperate rather than compete with other clubs. I realize this will require some re-thinking, but strategic cooperation could actually reduce competition and bring success to everyone in the end.

Fritz: (enthusiastic)
That's an entirely new perspective! Just think of the possibilities! We could establish an employee-exchange-program and bring new blood along with new ideas into the clubs.

Penny:
Not to mention the increase in motivation this might mean for employees who would enjoy working in a country where we don't have a club.

Jonathan: (leaning back in his chair)
This is definitely something we'll have to consider. I believe it has a lot of potential.
Ms. Saladino, what about our target groups? As a marketing expert and our newest sales director, I'd appreciate hearing your thoughts.

Adriana: (sitting up straighter in her chair)
Well, I tend to think more target-group rather than product-oriented. Our target group is comprised of people who have the same problems or needs.
In defining the group, we have to be very specific. We can then figure out the best way to fulfill their needs.

James:
That requires constant feedback from our customers, doesn't it?

Adriana: (nodding)
Absolutely. Maintaining a constant dialogue with our target group is a real learning process for us.
Any plans for improvement should be based on the needs of our customers.

James:
Whereas, I believe, it's important to concentrate on the basic and not the variable needs of the customer.

Adriana:
Yes. Basic needs remain constant and are something we can integrate into our corporate strategy more easily.

José Aquilar (Spanish Sales Director):
In my opinion, the only constant is change. We have to be ready for anything.

Jonathan:
Just what did you have in mind Mr. Aquilar?
As our financial whizz, I'd be very curious to hear about it.

José: (choosing his words carefully)
Well, take management trends for example.
Total Quality Management, Lean Production and Just-in-Time could mean big changes for all of us. We just have to be quicker than our competition in making use of these ideas.
I've noticed that it's not necessarily the larger companies who dominate the smaller ones. It's the company that adapts most quickly to change that wins in the end.

James:

Hmm, so much for the story about the tortoise and the hare. But I think that ties in well with what everyone has contributed to the meeting so far.

Jonathan: (nodding)

I quite agree. As a matter of fact, I've found every point made very useful in formulating our new corporate strategy. Penny, could you briefly summarize the points for us?

Penny: (reaching for her note pad)

Certainly, Sir.
1. Identify your greatest strengths and make use of them.
2. Be unique.
3. Be innovative.
4. Cooperate instead of competing with the competition.
5. Think target group rather than product-oriented.
6. Concentrate on the basic rather than the variable needs of the customer and
7. Adapt quickly to change.

Jonathan:

Very good. Thank you, Penny. Now that we've set the criteria for our new corporate strategy, I'd suggest we let it settle in our minds and continue after lunch. This meeting is now adjourned.

UNIT 2

One month has passed since the corporate strategy meeting at Sun Club headquarters in London. As a potential joint venture partner, William Garfield, an elderly, distinguished-looking man with white hair, has arrived from the Virgin Islands for negotiations. Wearing a light linen suit and beige canvas shoes, his tanned skin completes the impression of a man who has just returned from a cruise. He is the owner of a hotel complex called "Paradise Cove Hideaway" on the island of St. John.

Because Mr. Garfield's arrival was on a Friday, Jonathan and James invited him to play several rounds of golf over the weekend. This was an excellent way to get to know each other before beginning negotiations.

It is now Monday morning and Penny has just joined the three gentlemen seated at the mahogony table of the conference room.

Penny:
Good morning gentlemen. I hope you had a nice time playing golf the past two days. I'm sorry I couldn't join you.

James:
So are we Penny. We certainly had excellent weather for it. Penny, I'd like you to meet Mr. William Garfield. Mr. Garfield, this is my assistant, Ms. Penny McCloud.

Bill:
Please, call me Bill. It's a pleasure to finally meet you face-to-face, Penny. Your help in setting up this meeting was invaluable.

Penny:
Oh, the pleasure is mine. But I think it was really a stroke of luck Mr...umm... Bill. My family has known Mr. McBride, one of your regular guests, for over 30 years. When he told us that you were looking for potential investors in order to expand, I just put two and two together.

Jonathan:
And we're very happy you did, Penny. The hotel complex with its idyllic setting is just what Sun Club is looking for.

James:
Not to mention the beautiful sunsets we enjoyed during our visit there last month. All of our club locations offer great sunsets. It's become our trademark.

Bill:
Well, I'm happy to hear our complex fulfills so many of your requirements at first sight.

Penny:
Oh, before we begin, would anyone like some coffee or tea?

Bill:
Yes. I'll have some coffee with cream and sugar, please.

Jonathan:
Black for me, as usual, Penny.

Penny:
And plain hot water for you, right James?

James:
Yes, thanks Penny.

As Penny leaves the room to get the coffee, Bill leans towards James and says:

Bill:
I've never seen red hair like Penny's before.
It glows like fire.

James:
Yes, it's as beautiful as one of your sunsets, isn't it?

Bill: (leans back laughing)
You're right. I was wondering what I could compare it with.

Jonathan, who has been listening to the conversation, joins them in smiling his appreciation for Penny as she enters the room and sets the cups of coffee and boiled water on the table.

Bill:
Thank you very much, Penny.

UNIT 2

As Penny smiles, Bill turns to James and says:
Just plain boiled water, James? I could hardly believe my eyes when I saw you order it at the golf club yesterday.

Jonathan: (laughing)
Yes, that's just one of the many interesting habits James acquired during his travels. This particular one comes from China, I believe.

James:
Quite right. At first I thought the Chinese were only saving the cost of adding coffee or tea to their water. Then I discovered that plain hot water actually helps the digestion.

Bill:
Hmm. I'd be interested in hearing more about that during lunch. But now it's business before pleasure, right?

Jonathan:
Yes, I agree. Although our preliminary talks on St. John went very well, we've still got a lot to discuss. Our objective today should be to put down any agreements we come to in a **letter of intent**.

Bill:
I think you're right. I'd like to make the most out of my property before I retire. I've invested a lot of time and money in my life's work. This hotel is a part of me and there are many details that still have to be worked out to my personal satisfaction.

James:
We understand this aspect, Bill. We appreciate your personal **commitment** and feel it is one of the qualities that has made your hotel so successful. Nevertheless, if negotiations go well, we could help make you a very happy pensioner someday.

Bill: (chuckling)
I hope so.

Jonathan:
Fine. Then let's briefly review some of the items we've already talked about and elaborate on them. Penny, would you like to begin?

UNITS 28

Penny:
As we all know, St. John is the smallest of the U.S. Virgin Islands. It's only 28 square miles in size. Two thirds of the island has been declared a national park. Understandably, the local zoning law prohibits the building of any new tourist resorts. Only the expansion of already existing property is allowed.

James:
This has been a blessing in disguise for us. Our research has shown that although renovation will be costly, the founding of a joint venture with your hotel will be much cheaper than building a new one.

Bill:
In other words, I supply the property and you provide the capital to upgrade the existing structures.

Jonathan:
That's correct. It would greatly reduce our initial investment costs. But we would like to expand and install additional facilities in order to meet our club standards as well.

Bill:
I foresee no problems with expansion. There's still plenty of unused land on my property and the bureaucracy in the Virgin Islands doesn't involve much red tape. If we submit a well-defined building proposal to the respective authorities, we can expect to receive a building permit within two months.

James:
Excellent. Cooperation from the local authorities would be a great help. And we have no doubt that using local raw materials, equipment and labor will keep production costs at a minimum.

Bill:
I fully agree, plus any additional supplies we might need can easily be shipped from the United States. That way we'll be able to avoid customs expenses.

Jonathan:
This all sounds very promising. Now let's move on to some essential questions Penny still has open.

UNITS 30

Penny:
Thank you. In addition to the blueprints of the existing structures, we still need an inventory list of the assets you'll be bringing into the joint venture, Bill. Sun International can then have the value of your property assessed. This will help determine the percentage of each party's investment in the joint venture.

Bill:
Of course. I already have someone working on that list and should be able to fax it to you by next week. Today I've brought the tax statements of the last five years with me. They show that the property has depreciated at a rate of 5% per annum. I've also talked to my local bank and they would be willing to finance additional loans at a very favorable interest rate.

Jonathan:
Very good. We'll be examining this question in more detail later on.

Penny:
I'm looking forward to receiving your fax. In the meantime, I'll make a list of any further information we need as our negotiations progress. Sun International will then work on a feasibility study for the first five years of operation as a joint venture. I'll keep you informed every step of the way.

Bill:
I'd appreciate that. Perhaps we could turn to another matter now. On the fairway yesterday, we started to discuss the existing workforce of the hotel. I'd like to keep all of the staff.

Jonathan:
I'm afraid I can't agree with you there. Dependent upon the results of our feasibility study, we may have to let some of them go.

Bill: (shaking his head)
That's out of the question! I've been running a family business here. I wouldn't feel good about loyal employees losing their jobs. I have a certain responsibility for them and their families.

Jonathan:
You have a point there. I know we discussed taking over existing personnel, but Sun Club's major contribution to this project will be management and

marketing know-how. This means it's our job to determine the optimum number of staff needed to run the business efficiently.

Bill: (hesitantly)
Mmm, I'm not so sure. I'm not quite convinced yet.

James:
Perhaps we can find a compromise, Bill. I suggest we put Sun Club personnel in some key management positions, take over the rest of the existing workforce and then determine who stays after the first year of operation.

Bill:
So what you're really saying is, some people will get the "golden parachute" right away?

Penny: (looking perplexed)
Golden parachute? I'm sorry, but I'm not familiar with that expression.

James:
It's another way of referring to severance pay, Penny. A very visual expression. Yes, Bill. I think it could work this way. After all, a decrease in the workforce might result in an increase in productivity. It's worth a try.

Bill:
Well, maybe you're right. I tend to get too personally involved in my business and sometimes that stands in the way of making a profit I suppose.

James:
In my opinion, getting personally involved is more of an advantage than a disadvantage, Bill. Rest assured that we'll try to find solutions that will make everyone happy. It won't be easy but it's in both of our interests.

Bill:
Alright. If you put it that way, I think I could live with that.

Everyone breathes a **deep sigh of relief**. Before the meeting is **adjourned** for lunch, Penny sums up the main points that have been agreed upon. This gives both parties a chance to review their progress and clarify any misunderstandings that might **jeopardize** the success of the negotiations.

Winter has come to London. It is cold and windy outside and ominous grey clouds are hanging low over the city. Penny looks up from her desk as she hears the first drops of rain hitting the window. "Oh, wouldn't it be nice to be lying on a warm sunny beach in the Virgin Islands right now?" she thinks to herself.

The soothing sound of waves rolling onto the white sandy beach mixes with the cries of seagulls flying out over the surf. Penny squints and then shades her eyes to get a better look at the handsome waiter who is approaching with a round silver tray. Dressed in an elegant black vest and slacks, he greets her with a smile of his pearly white teeth. As he bends down to let her take an icecold cocktail glass filled with a red fruit drink, she can hear the ice cubes clinking against the side of the glass. She raises the glass to her lips and is just about to take a sip of the cool refreshing liquid...

James: (singing)
"What a day for a daydream..."

As James continues humming a few bars of the song, Penny's eyes fly open and she turns to find James standing in front of her desk grinning.

Penny:
Oh, James! You startled me. Yes, you're right. I was just looking out of the window, dreaming about the Virgin Islands.
My report for the feasibility study is almost finished. But on a day like today, I'd rather be gathering information first-hand on a beach in St. John instead of looking through the brochures sent by their Chamber of Commerce.

James:
Yes, I can imagine that. I'd love to join you on a beach there right now. Do you think anyone would notice if we just slipped out of the office for a few days?

Penny:
Hmm, let's dream on for a second. But seriously, I'm so glad negotiations for the joint venture went so well with Mr. Garfield. I never expected a rough draft of the contract could be agreed upon so quickly.

James:
Neither did I. I believe Bill will be a good joint venture partner in the long run. Very few details are left to be ironed out, thanks to his insight and your great investigative work.

Penny:
Not to mention your diplomacy. At times I was worried we would lose him.

James:
Let's face it. Together we make a great team, Penny. What would I do without you?

Penny: (smiling)
Probably eat too much chocolate. By the way, I picked up a bag of your favorite brand, with raisins of course.

James:
You're a life-saver, Penny. I'll try not to let it melt in my shirt pocket this time. It made such a mess during my business trip to the Islands. Not to mention the embarassment.

Penny:
Well, according to the information I've been gathering, the average temperature there is 25 degrees centigrade all year round. I'm not at all surprised your chocolate melted.

James:
Yes, but there was always a nice breeze blowing. St. John is very romantic and undeveloped.
It has no crowds or traffic, whereas St. Thomas is quite a cosmopolitan Caribbean port.

Penny:
That confirms what I've read. They say, "St. John is the Virgin Islands' most virgin." Since two thirds of the island is a national park, the natural beauty and wildlife can be enjoyed by everyone. It seems their government takes environmental protection very seriously.

James:
Surely being a U.S. territory has influenced their economic and social as well as their environmental policy. Industrial nations know they are responsible for producing a high proportion of global pollution.

Penny:
Yes, I'm certain an increasing number of businesses realize environmentalism is an important issue for them in the '90's.
Our project is a good example. Efficient energy use in insulation, air-conditioning and lighting are just a few of the measures that have top priority during expansion work on the club. Proper water conservation and waste disposal are additional areas for concern.

James:
I'm glad Sun Club is ecology-minded. Doing all that's economically viable to protect the environment now will put us a step ahead of the competition, should the government set stricter environmental standards in the future.

Penny:
The information I gathered about the political system and the economy on the Islands is fascinating. I didn't know that everyone born on the U.S. Virgin Islands is automatically a United States citizen.

James:
Yes, but apparently the islands only have one delegate in the U.S. House of Representatives, who isn't even entitled to vote.

Penny:
That's correct. Jurisdiction lies in the hands of district courts and a governor is voted into office every two years.

James:
I've been told the crime rate is low and that there are few social problems on the Islands. Although it's not supposed to be an affluent society, from what I observed, the standard of living seems fairly high.

Penny:
That's interesting. According to these statistics, there's been a decrease in the resident population since 1985. This helped to cut the unemployment rate in

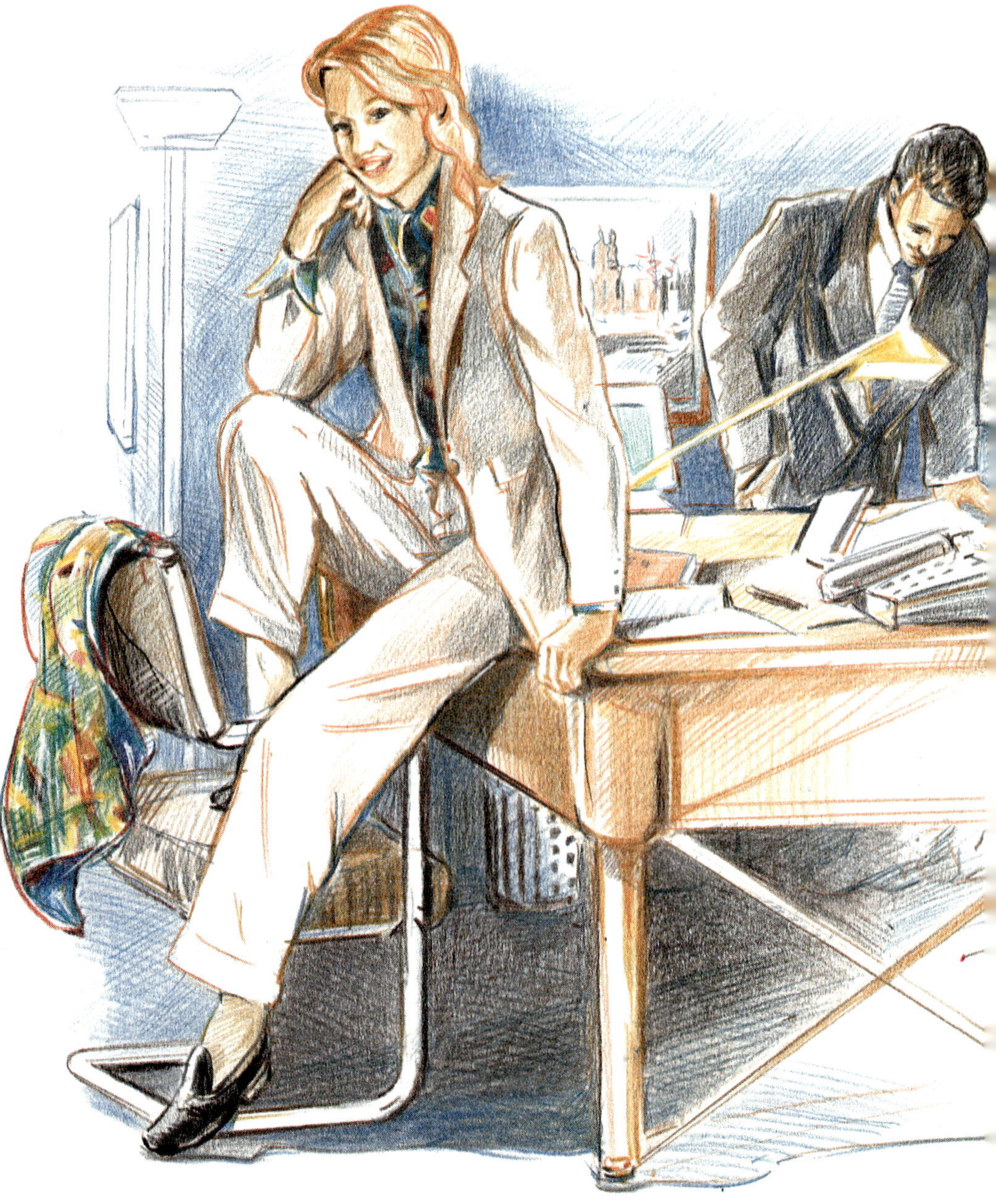

half. But Bill mentioned the local politicians are very happy about our plans for expansion. With over 1.8 million visitors yearly, the tourist industry has played a major role in providing jobs for skilled as well as unskilled labor.
The St. Johnians, which is how people born on the island refer to themselves, are mainly of African descent. A cultural mix from other Caribbean islands, along with continentals from the U.S. mainland make up the rest of the population.

James:
Do they still produce rum and export it like they used to? I can imagine sailing the turquoise-colored seas like the notorious pirates Blackbeard or Captain Kidd, attacking ships laden with precious treasure.

Penny: (laughing)
Sure, I can just picture you with a patch over one eye, a squawking parrot on your shoulder and a ring dangling from your ear: "James The Terrible".
Now please, let me get back to work. Your plane ticket to Madrid was delivered this morning, but I still need to change those travel arrangements for your meeting scheduled with Fritz in Frankfurt.

James:
Okay, Penny. Enough adventure for today!

As James walks out the door, Penny shakes her head and smiles, amused. She pushes her paperwork aside and opens a drawer on the left-hand side of her desk. Taking out a file marked "Travel", she reaches for the phone. After punching the memory button for the stored number of an airline, she hears a few rings before a male voice answers.

Reservations agent:
British Airways reservations. May I help you?

Penny:
Yes, this is Penny McCloud, Sun International, speaking. I'd like to cancel a reservation made under the following booking code: JB1ROH / 6A.

Reservations agent:
That was a reservation made for a Mr. James Thorne.

Penny:
That's correct. I'd like to make a new booking for him now, please. According to your timetable, there's a daily flight departing from London Heathrow to Frankfurt, Germany at 7 a.m. Do you still have space available in business class on January 15th?

Reservations agent:
No, I'm sorry. I'm afraid that flight is fully booked. I can offer him a seat in business class at 8 a.m., however.

Penny:
Well, he has to be at a meeting by 11:15 and Germany is one hour ahead of us. If his arrival time is 10:30 that won't give him enough time to reach his final destination.

Reservations agent:
If he's only travelling with hand luggage, he should be able to make a quick connection with the train located underneath the airport. That will get him into downtown Frankfurt within 20 minutes.

Penny:
Hmm, perhaps they can start the meeting a bit later, just in case. Alright then, I'll take that seat. And I'd like to book the return for the following day at 6 p.m.

Reservations agent:
I can confirm that. Your new booking reference is DT3KWA / 1F. The ticket can be picked up or sent to you with the invoice.

Penny:
Fine. We'll pick it up when the time comes. Thank you very much. Good-bye.

Reservations agent:
Thank you for calling British Airways. Goodbye.

Penny hangs up and starts to flip through the yellow pages of her phone book. She finds the toll-free number of an international hotel chain and punches it into her receiver. After two rings a female voice answers.

Hotel reservations agent:
Good afternoon, Executive Lodges. How may I help you?

Penny:
Hello. This is Penny McCloud, Sun International, speaking. I'd like to reserve a room at your hotel in Frankfurt, Germany, please.

Hotel reservations agent:
What is the arrival date and for how many persons would you like the room, please?

Penny:
We need a non-smoking, single room for the night of January 15th. It should be booked under the name Thorne, James Thorne.

Hotel reservations agent:
You're in luck. The International Textile fair ends on that day so we have rooms opening up again. Although we only have a double room available, we'll charge him the single rate. Will he be staying just the one night?

Penny:
Yes, that's right. What is the single room rate?

Hotel reservations agent:
After subtracting your corporate discount of 25 per cent, it will come to DM 180 for the night.

Penny:
Fine. Mr. Thorne will be paying by credit card when he arrives. Thank you very much.

Hotel reservations agent:
You're welcome. Thank you for calling Executive Lodges Worldwide. Bye.

Penny spends the next half hour rescheduling appointments for James, who has been asked to make a trip to Madrid on short notice. On the verge of signing the joint venture contract, everyone working on the feasibility study wants to double-check their facts. Finished for the day, Penny closes the file and covers the keyboard of her personal computer as she flips the switch to turn it off. Outside the rain has stopped and the sun is trying to peek through the clouds.

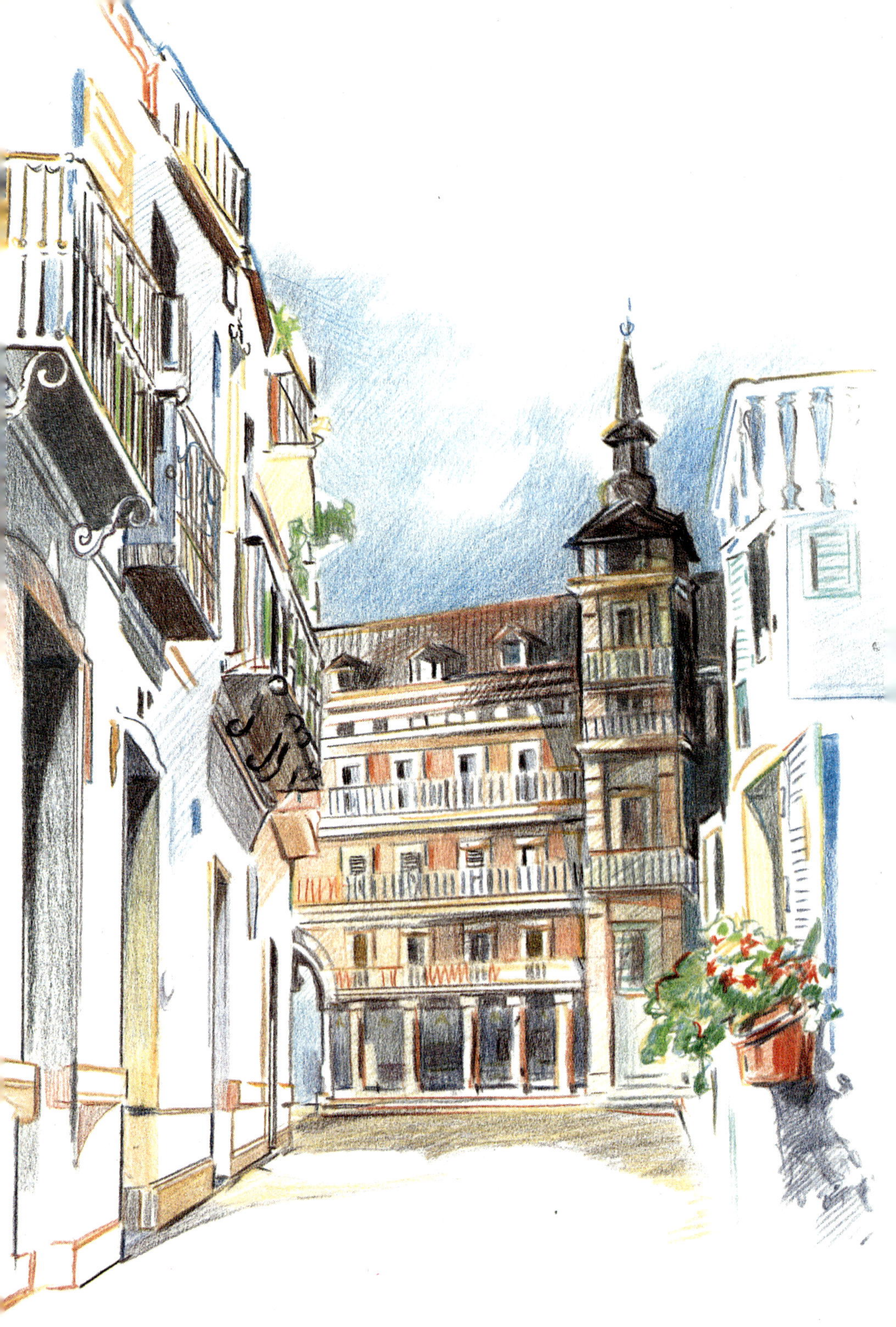

Although the air is crisp, a sunny, blue sky greets James upon his arrival in Madrid. As his white taxi weaves its way through the traffic from the airport to a glass office tower not far from the Prado museum, sounds of the city, mixed with excerpts of Spanish conversation, reach his ears. He smiles, fondly remembering the two years he spent here during his childhood. An athletic-looking man wearing a pink shirt and trendy tie under a forest-green suit, is waiting for James. His jet-black hair is combed straight back from his forehead. At the age of 28, José Aquilar is the youngest of Sun Club's sales directors. He is in charge of the Spain office. As a financial whizz, he has also been given the task of preparing a report for the feasibility study. During his research on Mr. Garfield's financial background, he discovered something he thinks James should know. The two of them are now seated at a table located in one corner of José's bright, spacious office.

James:
I assume you've received all the records and financial statements Penny forwarded to you on Mr. Garfield's operation.

José: (nodding)
Yes, almost everything I needed.
The balance sheet as of December 31st, itemized the fixed and current assets as well as the liabilities.
In addition to cash, inventories and receivables, Mr. Garfield has some stocks and bonds that can be added to his current assets.

James:
During our negotiations, he mentioned that he didn't want to liquidate his securities in order to fund an expansion. That was lucky for us. What about his fixed assets?

José: (holding a piece of paper)
Well, the balance sheet indicates the accumulated depreciation on the value of the buildings, furniture and fixtures. This includes all equipment attached to the buildings such as lighting, plumbing, heating and air-conditioning.

James:
And what about the land?

José:
Although the land is a fixed asset, it's value doesn't decline and therefore shows no depreciation.

James:
Am I correct in assuming the depreciation schedule is a part of the income tax law of the Virgin Islands?

José:
Yes, you're right, James. I've also cleared up some additional questions I had with Mr. Garfield's accountant. Current liabilities include accrued sales and payroll taxes as well as the income tax.
Mr. Garfield also has some debts to a bank which supplied him with a short-term credit and a company which installed a new refrigeration system.

James:
Does he have any long-term liabilities?

José:
His only long-term liability is a mortgage on the property. It carries a low interest rate of 6.4% and is scheduled to be paid off at the end of this year.

James:
Has he borrowed money or taken out a loan for anything else connected to the business?

José: (shaking his head)
Not to my knowledge. After subtracting his debts from his assets, my analysis of the balance sheet reveals Paradise Cove Hideaway to be in sound financial condition. I'll fax my report on the net worth of the enterprise to the feasibility study team tomorrow.

James:
Fine. But you said you discovered something important you wanted to speak to me about in person. You've made me very curious, José.

José: (leaning back)
It's probably nothing, but when dealing with money, my motto has always been "better safe than sorry".

James:
I fully agree with you. Tell me, is there something about Mr. Garfield's background we should know?

José: (leaning forward again)
Well, during my investigative work I went far back into Mr. Garfield's past. At one time he owned a small resort on the eastern coast of the Gulf of Mexico. After three years of operation, it went bankrupt.
The bankruptcy proceedings divided the estate up and settled the wage and salary claims first. Then the other debts were paid. Because Mr. Garfield and his partner had set up an unlimited company, they were liable without restriction. They lost all of their personal property in the process.

James: (looking relieved)
Good work, José. It's important for us to base our decisions on complete information. But let me ease your worries. Losing the resort was not Mr. Garfield's fault.

José: (surprised)
But, how do you know?

James:
It's my job to know, remember? After Mr. Garfield mentioned a financial failure to us while we were playing golf, I did some investigative work of my own. During the winter of his third tourist season, a severe storm caused an oil tanker to run aground. There was a massive oil spill which affected the coastline for 50 miles south of the accident.

José:
But why didn't I read anything about it?

James:
In those days, environmental accidents weren't publicized as they are today. The oil business was booming in Texas and created a lot of jobs. Nobody was going to complain about a little oil spill.

José:
Ah, nobody but Mr. Garfield, right? I assume his property was affected by the spill.

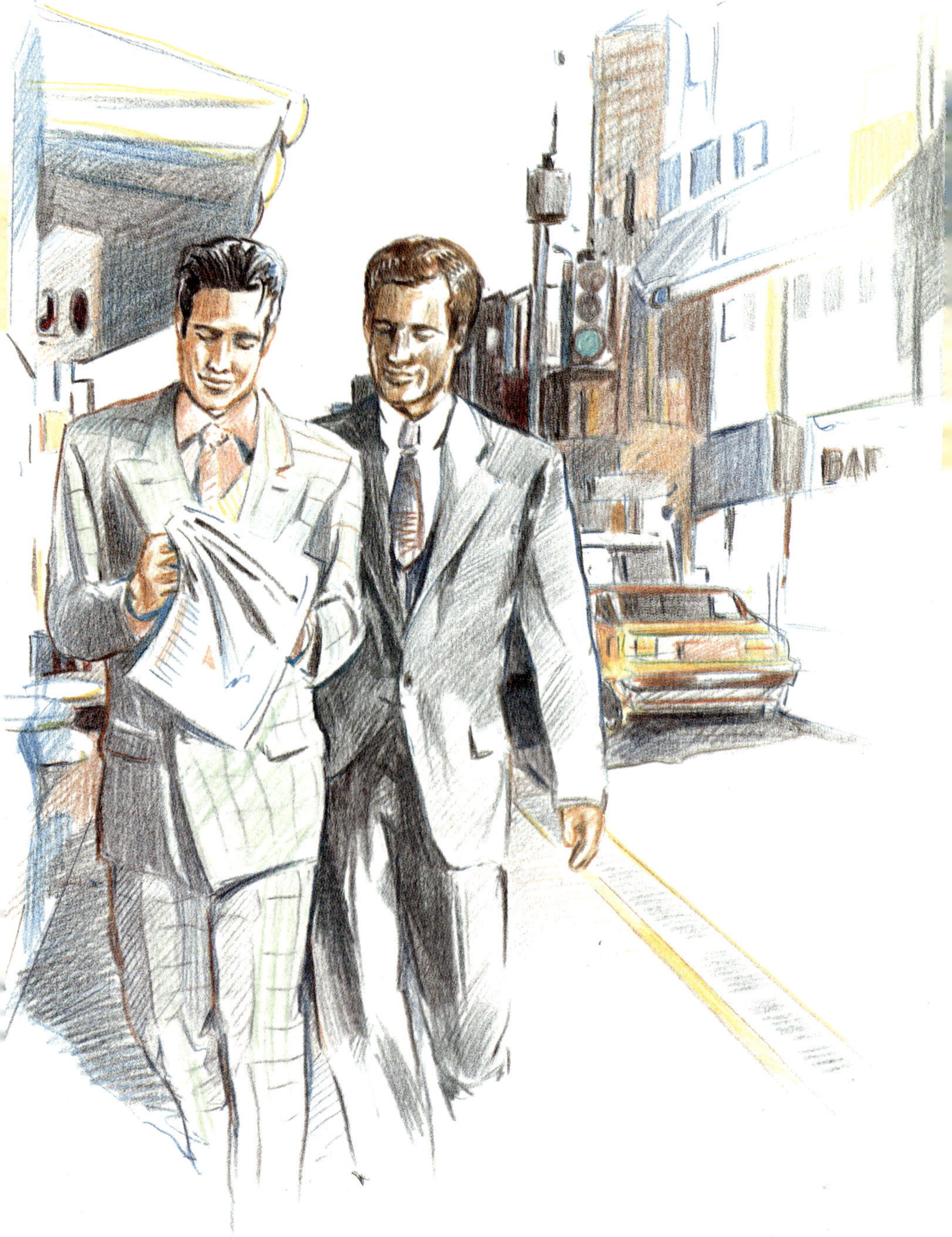

James:
Exactly. The beach looked like a disaster area but there were no clean-up crews and no financial aid to be expected from the state.
It happened during peak season. Most of Mr. Garfield's guests broke off their vacations and future guests cancelled their reservations. The season was ruined for him and he was never able to recover from the loss.

José:
But wasn't he insured against such an event occuring?

James: (shaking his head)
No. People didn't place much value in insurance in those days.
It never even occured to Mr. Garfield and his partner that such a thing could happen.

José:
Aha, so he was probably under-insured and what little insurance he had in no way covered the costs, right?

James: (nodding)
Right.
Important for us was to determine whether the bankruptcy was a case of mismanagement on Mr. Garfield's part or not. I'm convinced that under the circumstances, it could have happened to anyone.

José: (knitting his brow)
But that still leaves me with one question.
If he was financially ruined, how did Mr. Garfield have the money to buy property and start building a hotel in the Virgin Islands just a few years later?

James:
I knew you'd ask that. His parents, who were quite wealthy, died in a plane crash. Being an only child, William Garfield inherited everything. It was his dream to become self-employed again. He wasted no time in taking the money and moving to St. John.

José:
It sounds like a fairy-tale.

James:
Most success stories do. Working out the budget for our expansion plans might be your next challenge, José. So don't worry, be happy. We've got a good partner here.

José: (laughing)
Okay, if you say so.

James:
Now please, tell me where the nearest bank is. I still have to cash a traveller's check before it closes.

José gives James directions on how to get to a bank which is located right around the corner. Upon entering, James spots a beautiful woman with long dark hair sitting behind a glass window.
He recognizes the Spanish word for 'Exchange' and is pleased that she is sitting directly below the sign. He walks over to the counter and stops in front of her.

Bank teller: (with a friendly smile)
May I help you?

James:
Yes, I hope so. I'd like to change some money.

Teller:
Do you want to change cash or checks?

James: (reaching for a pen)
I'd like to cash this traveller's check and I'd also like to exchange these American dollars for pesetas.

Teller:
Could I see some identification, please?

James: (reaching into his breastpocket)
Of course. Here is my passport. It has a very up-to-date photo in it. I'm sure you'll recognize me.

Teller: (giggling)
Oh, but it doesn't do you justice at all. Then again, most passport photos look nothing like their owners.

James: (feigning concern)
I believe you're right. Will you take care of the transaction for me anyway?

Teller:
Yes, this is your lucky day. I've forgotten my glasses.

James: (laughing)
I'm so glad. What is today's exchange rate?

Teller: (handing James a printout)
Here are the current exchange rates listed for pounds and dollars into pesetas. How would you like your bills?

James:
In smaller notes and a little bit of change, please. I'd like to do some shopping this evening.

Teller:
It's lovely weather for it. Here you are.

The teller counts the money out loud as she lays it down on the counter in front of him.

Teller:
Please recount it to be sure it's the correct amount.

James:
Oh, but I trust you completely, even if you aren't wearing your glasses today.

They both have a grin on their faces as James thanks her and turns to leave.

Teller:
Oh, you've forgotten your passport Mr. Torne!

James: (turning back)
That's Thorne, James Thorne. Thank you so much. By the way, would you like to join me for some dinner and shopping this evening? I have to find a birthday gift for a friend and perhaps you could help me.

Teller: (pleasantly surprised)
Why, yes. I'd love to. The bank closes at 2 p.m. today but I have to do some paperwork until five o'clock.

James:
Fine. I'll pick you up then, okay? We can stroll over to the Plaza Major and begin our shopping spree there.

She agrees and James leaves the bank, happy for the chance to practise his Spanish with a charming new acquaintance.

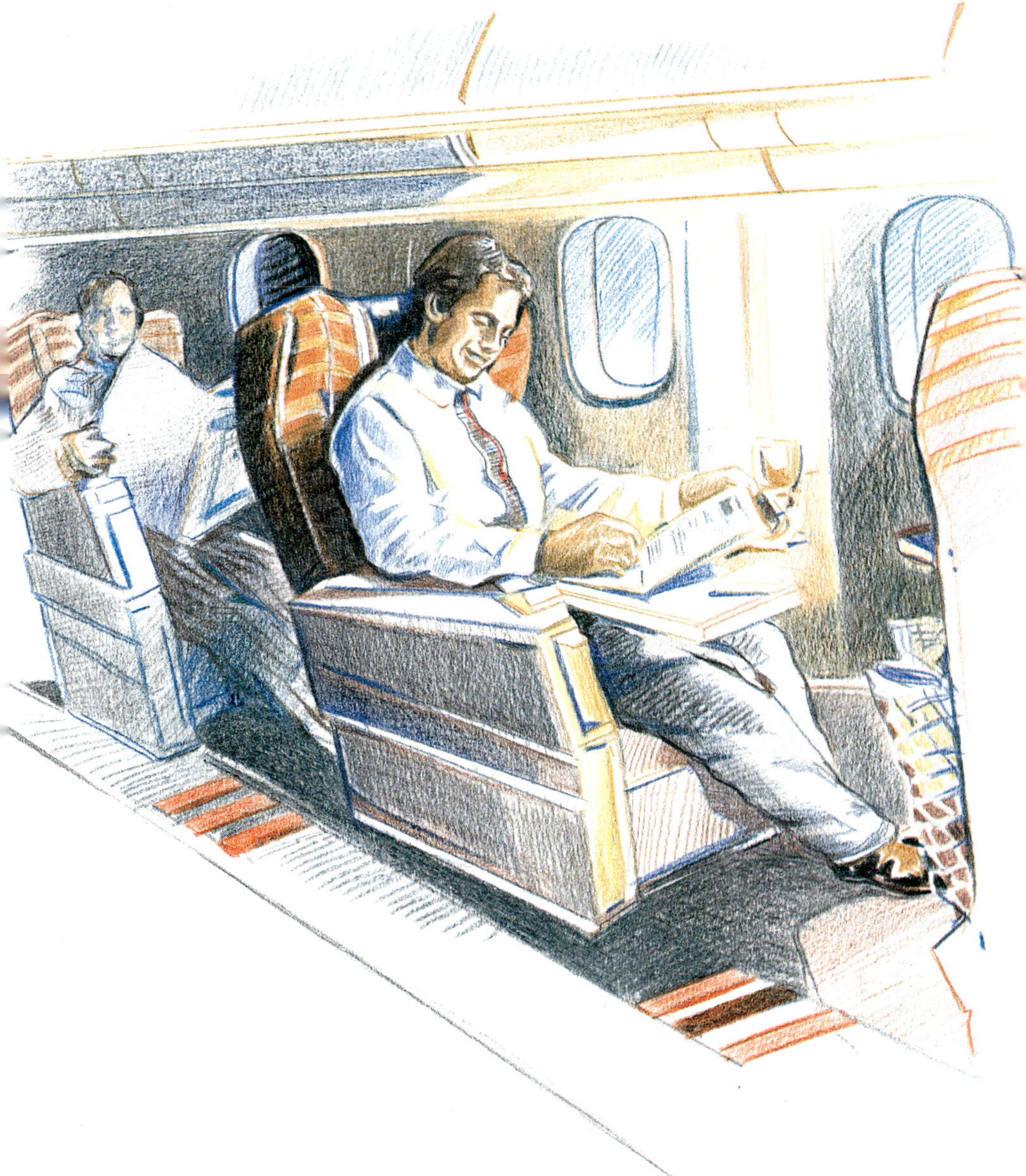

5

As James' plane is flying in a holding pattern over the Frankfurt airport, he munches on some chocolate-covered raisins and glances down at the cloud-covered city outside his window.

"Perhaps I'll rent a car instead of taking the train into town," he thinks to himself, as he sees the autobahn winding its way into the city.

Turning back to the curriculum vitae Fritz Fischer, the sales director of the Germany branch has sent him, he notices that he has left a chocolate fingerprint on each page. He takes a napkin and tries to repair the damage, but it's too late. Giving up, he resigns himself to the fact that it's not the first time this has happened and it probably won't be the last.

Once again he directs his attention to the folder in front of him. Through a headhunter, the personnel department has found a promising candidate for the position of club manager. Fritz has interviewed the candidate and believes he is perfect for the Virgin Islands club. In order to help make the final decision, James has also been asked to meet him.

The plane lands and James makes his way through immigration to the baggage claim area. Within minutes of spotting his small, leather suitcase, he is on his way to terminal A, where he knows the rental car-agencies are located. He approaches a young, blond, curly-haired man sitting behind a counter.

Rental car agent:
Hello. May I help you?

James: (putting down his suitcase)
Yes, I'd like to hire a BMW 320i until 5 p.m. tomorrow with pick-up and drop-off at the airport, please.

Agent: (looking at the screen of his terminal)
That would be our group C category. Oh, I'm terribly sorry sir, but we have no 320i's available at the moment. May I offer you a Mercedes C180 instead? The rate is the same and a car phone is included.

James:
Alright. That's fine. What else does the rate cover?

Agent:
The rate includes VAT, unlimited mileage and third-party insurance which will cover you against damage to another vehicle in case of an accident.

James:
How much more will it cost to have fully comprehensive insurance?

Agent:
If you wish to insure against damage to the rental car, a collision damage waiver is an additional fee of DM 18.00 per day.

James:
I'll take that also then.

Agent: (checking off items on the form)
Fine. May I see your driver's license, please? Will you be the only driver?

James: (handing him his license)
Yes, that's right.

Agent:
How would you like to pay that, Sir?

James:
By credit card, please.

The rental car agent takes care of the remaining formalities. Just as James walks through the sliding glass doors of the terminal, an assistant pulls up in a shiny, new, dark blue Mercedes. He hands the keys to James who has just stowed his suitcase in the trunk and is now making himself comfortable behind the steering wheel. Within minutes, James is on the autobahn, joining the traffic flowing into the city of Frankfurt. After finding a parking spot in a garage near the office, James hurries to his appointment with Fritz. A good-humored, slightly bald man, you can tell by Fritz's somewhat round proportions, that he enjoys eating good food. The prospective candidate, Otto Huber, on the other hand, is a tall, slim man in his thirties. He seems confident and at ease and James' first impression of him is quite positive. After introductions are made, the three begin with some small talk and then get down to business.

James: (with an encouraging smile)
Well Mr. Huber, as you probably already know from our executive search consultant, our short-list is down to two potentially suitable candidates. You're one of them.

Otto (looking pleased):
I'm very happy to hear that. It might take some persuasion to lure me away from my old company, but I must admit I am quite flattered.

James:
Your curriculum vitae and references are very impressive. Your background shows that you've not only managed several large hotels, but grew up in a family business as well.

Otto:
Yes, that's right. My parents still own a hotel in a ski area in the Swiss Alps. We always had many international guests and I received hands-on experience in every area of the business. In addition to my training at home, I completed my formal education in a college of hotel management.

James: (referring to the CV)
You then left home to take up your first position as Food and Beverage Manager of the Four Season's Hotel in Toronto, Canada.

Otto: (nodding)
Yes, I jumped at the chance to go to North America and was able to greatly improve my English while I was there.

James:
Hmm, I can hear that. Your pronunciation is excellent. I read here that you also speak Italian and French in addition to German. The ability to speak several European languages fluently, as well as good leadership qualities, is a prerequisite for this job.

Otto:
That's the advantage of growing up in Switzerland. As for leadership qualities, I've had the responsibility of guiding, influencing or supervising people to some degree since I was a teenager.

James: (turning to the second page)
According to your references, you're quite good at it. We're particularly interested in hearing about how you instituted aspects of Total Quality Management in the hotel you're presently employed with.

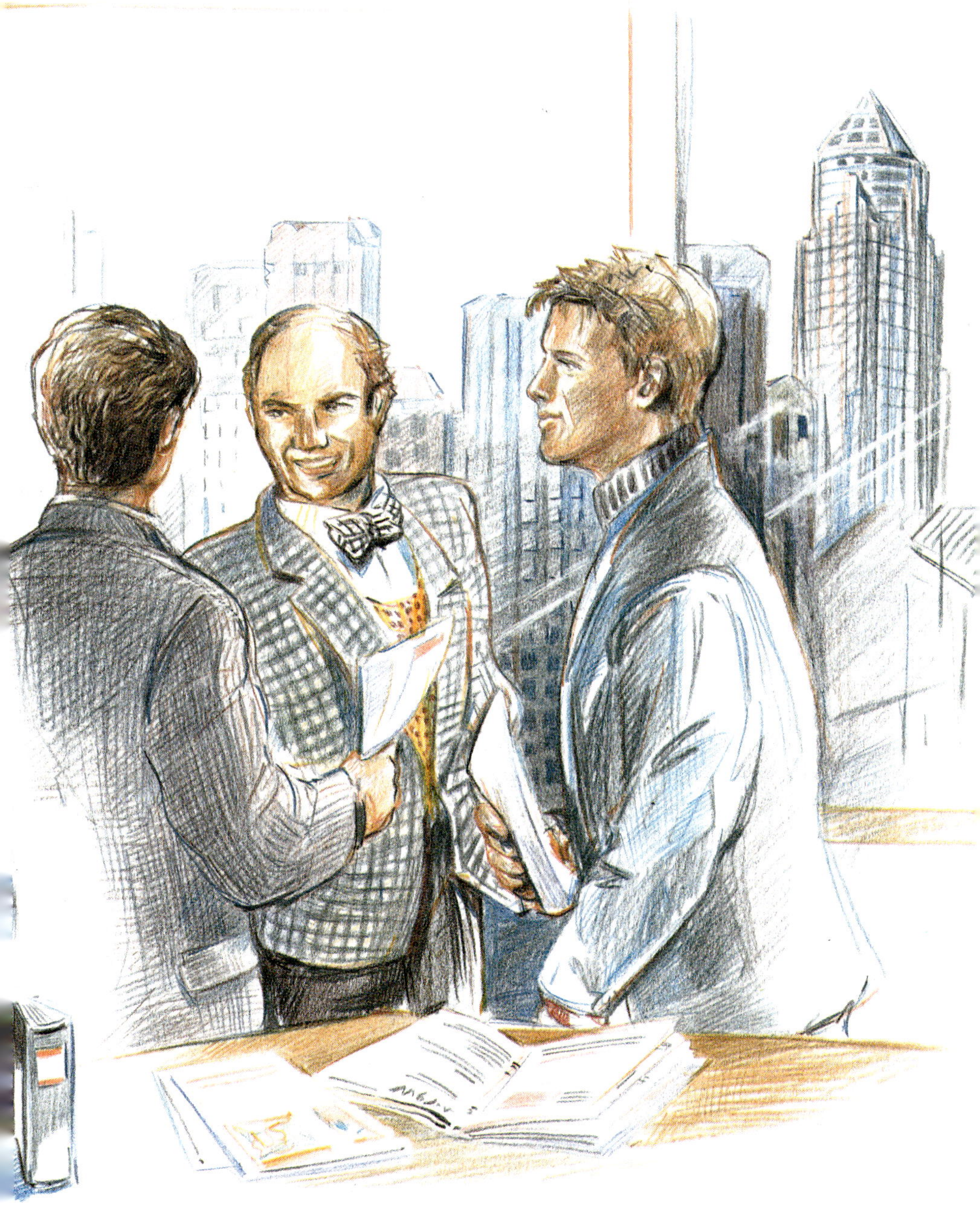

As Otto describes this new trend and how he implemented it, the interview continues in a relaxed atmosphere. The participants appear to feel very comfortable with one another. James appreciates Otto's modest, yet straight-forward style and can understand why Fritz is so enthusiastic about him.
Satisfied with what he has heard, James proceeds by describing the company structure to Otto.
Referring to the organizational chart of Sun International, Fritz joins James in explaining how the chart shows the relationship between the various levels of management and the staff.

James: (pointing to the top of the chart)
Four executives make up the Board of Directors followed by our CEO who oversees the Senior Executive Vice Presidents of the various divisions.

Otto:
Oh, so Sun Club isn't a subsidiary?

Fritz:
That's right. We're a division, which means we're a part of the company, and yet are still managed like a small enterprise.

James:
Next to the traditional departments most companies have, such as Sales, Finance and Human Resources, we have additional departments unique to our business. Sports and Entertainment is very important, along with Club Operations and Franchising.

Otto: (studying the hierarchy)
Who would be my superior according to this chart?

James:
You would report directly to Mr. Fischer, who is in charge of club management, as well as running our Germany office.

Otto:
Based on the information I've received from your personnel department and my interview with Mr. Fischer, the responsibilities of my position with Sun Club seem fairly clear to me. Naturally I'm also curious to know what the possibilities for advancement are within the company.

Fritz:
Well, the first step would be a lateral transfer from one club to another. As development planned over the next four years shows strategic growth, with the addition of six new clubs through franchising, joint ventures and construction, opportunities for a promotion will surely increase. Your performance, nevertheless, will dictate career progression within the company.

James:
The salary, as discussed with Mr. Fischer, would be complemented by generous fringe benefits. These include health insurance, a pension scheme, free accommodation in all our clubs and participation in a bonus plan based on personal and company performance.

Otto:
Would the health insurance cover both medical and dental costs?

Fritz:
Yes, of course. Relocation expenses will also be taken care of and 32 days of vacation are a part of the package.

James:
An intensive one-month training period will familiarize you with the company and our club philosophy.

Otto:
How long is the probationary period?

James:
A six-month probationary period begins once you take over your new position as General Manager of our U.S. Virgin Islands club.

Otto: (leaning back in his chair)
Well, I'm very interested at this point. I still have some questions about the Islands, but everything else I've heard makes me keen on joining your company. I hope I'm your man.

James and Fritz exchange glances and an unspoken understanding seems to pass between them.

James: (smiling)
It's not very difficult for us to make a commitment at this stage, Mr. Huber. After evaluating your qualifications, we'd like to welcome you on our team. A written offer will be sent to you by the end of next week.

Otto looks very happy as both Fritz and James move forward to shake his hand and congratulate him. There is an easy rapport between them and Fritz spontaneously makes a suggestion.

Fritz: (sounding elated)
I think we should celebrate! There's a great restaurant specializing in local food in a historic area of Frankfurt called Sachsenhausen. I could reserve a table for seven-thirty. How does that sound?

James:
Good idea! During dinner we can fill Otto in on the Islands. By the way, you don't mind my calling you by your first name, do you?

Otto: (waving it off with his hand)
Not at all. After having lived in Canada, I really prefer it. Shall we meet in the restaurant?

James:
My hotel is not far from Sachsenhausen. Why don't we meet there for Happy Hour at six o'clock first?

They all agree and Fritz offers to pick up Otto at his hotel on the way.

In the evening, the three men walk through the streets of Frankfurt. Although it is dark and cold outside, they are in a good mood, thanks to several "two for one" beers. With stomachs growling from hunger, they arrive in a cobblestone street lined with framework houses. Music floats out of the door of a pub as they pass by and enter the restaurant Fritz has suggested.
After a waiter shows them to their table and brings the menus, Fritz makes some recommendations on local specialties to try. The three of them settle down to a delicious dinner and an enjoyable night out on the town.

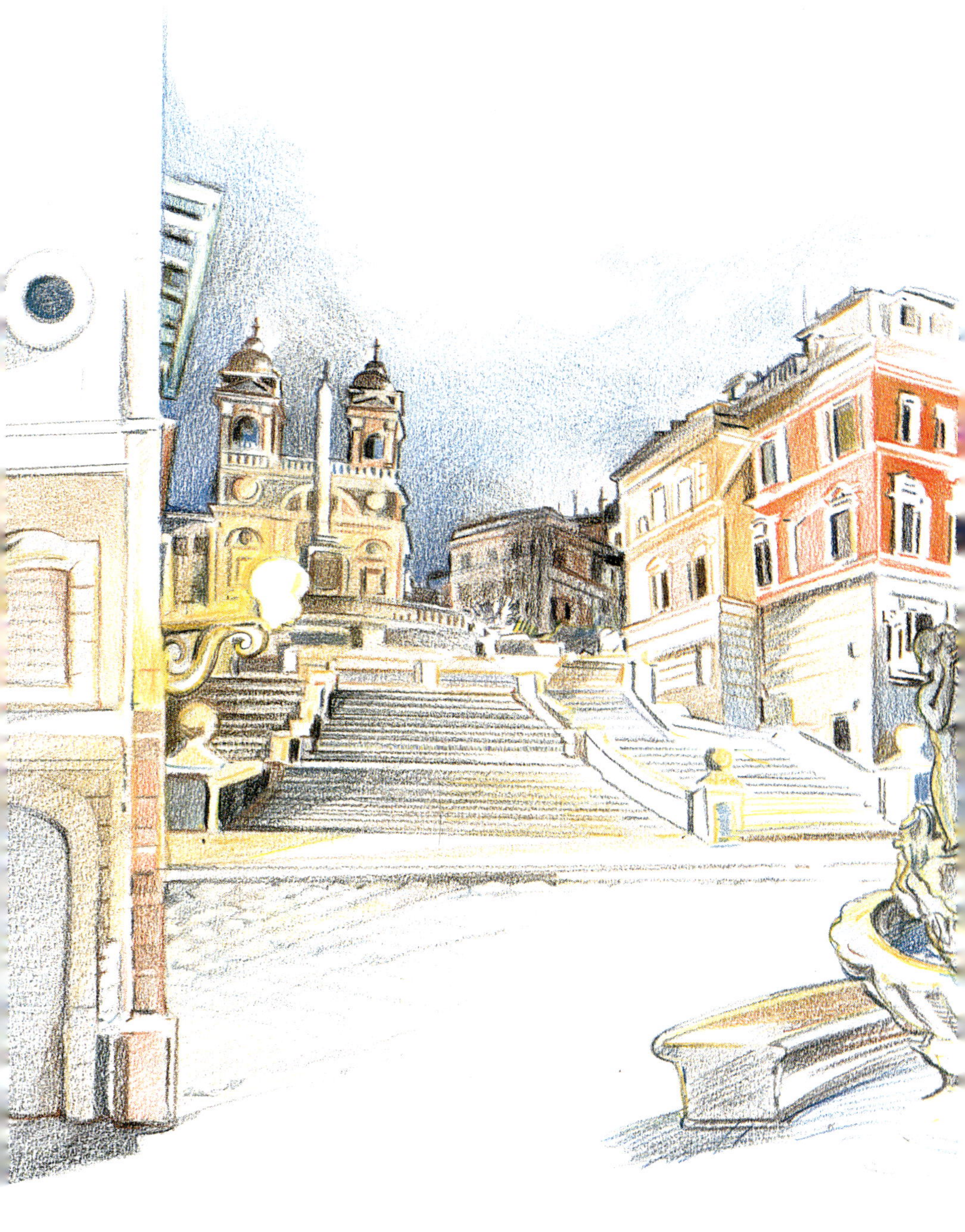

UNIT 6

The trees are in full bloom as spring spreads its warmth through the city of Rome. Chirping birds, church bells and the honking horns of rush hour traffic come together to create a strange music. The scent of flowers permeates the air as a warm breeze envelopes pedestrians on their way to work, causing them to inwardly unfold like petals reaching toward the sun.

On the east bank of the Tiber river, Sun Club's Italy branch office is located in the commercial section of the city. As James gazes out of the office window, he can pick out church domes and monuments between the Roman roof-gardens. Happy to have left a grey, foggy London behind, James is looking forward to discussing Sun Club's newest marketing strategy with its Italian sales director, Adriana Saladino. In her fashionable, designer outfit, Adriana looks younger than her 44 years. Her long black hair is intricately woven into a braid resting at the nape of her neck. She exhibits an exuberant personality as she sits down to discuss business with James.

Adriana:
It's so nice that you were able to come, James. Although our marketing strategy for the new club is progressing very well, I'm a little unsure about the advertising agency we should use for our ad campaign.

James:
Well, since you haven't been with the company for very long, I can understand your uncertainty. We have to handle our corporate image with care. Reputations can be tarnished quickly if unethical marketing activities are used.

Adriana:
That reminds me of some of the ads originating in Italy lately. Many of them have been very controversial. Personally, I find them innovative, but although we have a relatively open society, not everyone has such a liberal attitude.

James:
Fortunately, our logo is fairly unambiguous. It has international appeal and represents what we offer very clearly.

Adriana: *(with a daydreamy look)*
Hmm, "Sun", and a little fun to go along with it; something almost everyone yearns for. *(appearing businesslike once again)*
But, as you know, the real challenge in this campaign will be to add conference facilities to that offer without the negative connotation of work.

James:
Yes, you're right. Not an easy thing to accomplish. When is our appointment with the representative of the ad agency?

Adriana:
I've arranged a business luncheon at a restaurant not far from here. Mr. Gionelli has received the portfolio on our corporate identity and has been briefed on our project and what we're looking for.
Until then, we have time to discuss what the marketing department has worked on so far.

As James settles back to listen to her presentation, Adriana gestures with her hands a great deal as she describes the marketing study that was conducted in preparation for the campaign.

Adriana: (handing James a folder)
In an effort to define our marketing objectives, we first had to find out more about our target group. The study included questions about occupation, income, the level of education and the target's social class, whether it be working, middle or upper class.
Although we had a rough idea which market we would be aiming our advertising at, we wanted to be sure our product addresses the customer's needs.

James:
In other words, you want to offer our target group what they need most for their own development, thereby hitting them in the most effective spot, right?

Adriana: (looking a bit perplexed)
That's a very abstract way of putting it, but yes, I guess you could say that. By including business clientele in our research, we discovered that the addition of conference facilities in our clubs would solve their need for conducting a part of their business in a more relaxed atmosphere.

James: (putting the folder down)
I imagine the wave of management seminars offering time-planning, Neuro-linguistic Programming and meditation for managers fits into this concept nicely.

Adriana: (her eyes lighting up)
Hmm, I hadn't thought of that. But you're right. Consumer awareness has increased for courses of this kind and I think our clubs could provide just the right atmosphere. We'll have to check into its marketability.

James:
Good. What about the potentially lucrative market of incentive travel? I suppose that will play a vital role for us too.

Adriana: (nodding)
Definitely. That's a highly competitive market but we're willing to take the risk. More and more companies are offering non-cash incentives, like an all-expenses-paid holiday, as a performance-related reward to their employees. We should certainly cash in on this trend.

James:
Which means of advertising have you chosen?

Adriana:
Well, among the different forms of media available, we've decided against television commercials, radio and newspapers. These would be very costly forms of advertising.
We believe in a more direct approach. Our sales team will talk to company heads face-to-face, while distributing promotional literature and tasteful giveaways. This will be supplemented by direct mailings and full-page ads in business magazines.

James:
Have you considered using a celebrity endorsement in our advertising?

Adriana:
Yes, we have. We won't be using pop stars or movie actors. A successful, well-known head of a corporation or a world-class tennis or golf player would be more appropriate.

James: (contemplative)
Hmm, yes, I can imagine our target group could more easily identify with someone like that. I even have a few ideas of whom we could use to promote our product.

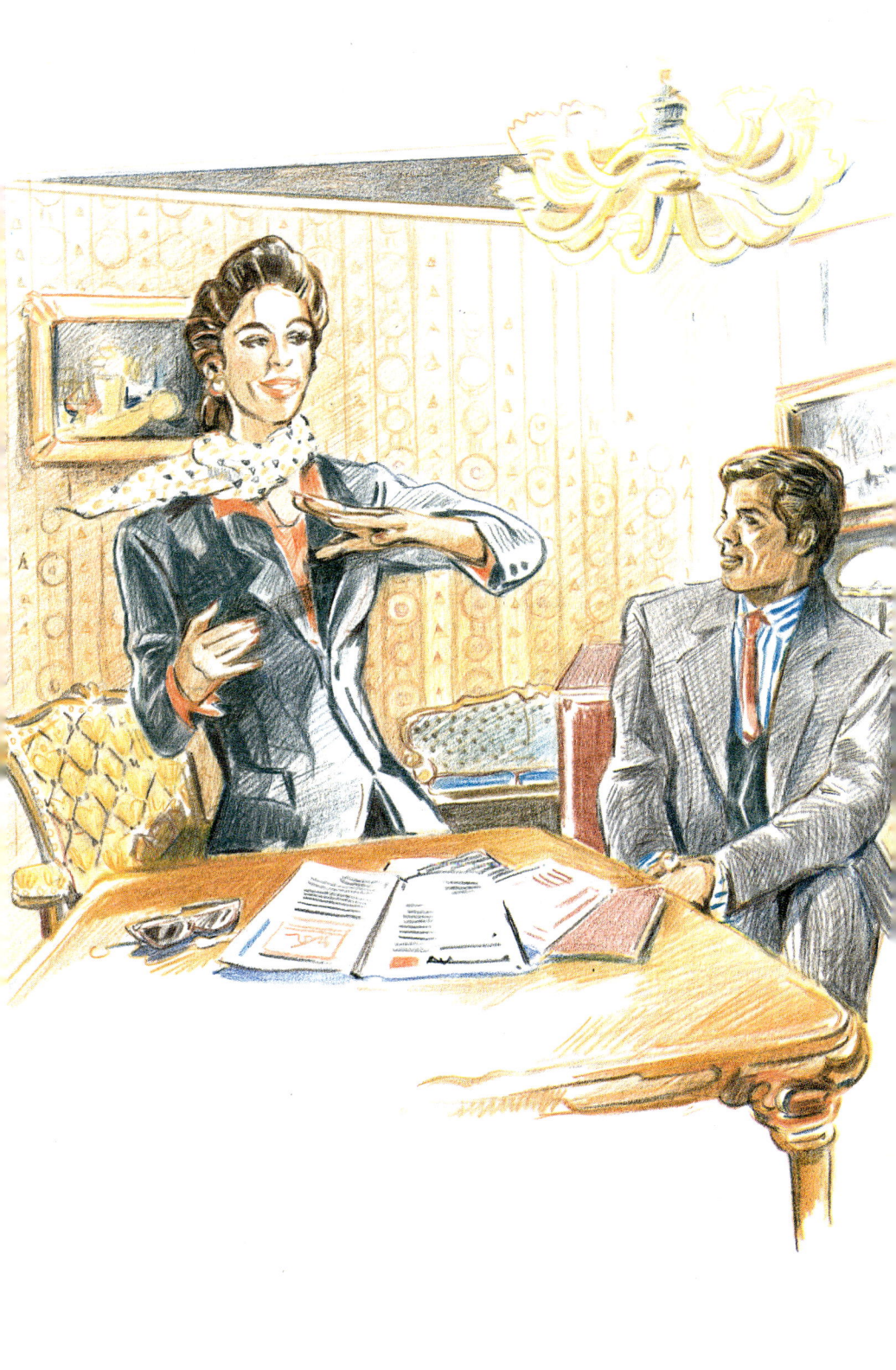

Adriana: (in an eager voice)
Great! I can hardly wait to hear about them! We can elaborate on this idea during our meeting with Mr. Gionelli. The clearer our concept is when we meet with him, the better.

James pours himself another cup of plain hot water from a teapot resting on a hotplate in one corner of Adriana's office. Amused, yet always ready to try something new, Adriana asks him to pour her a cup too.

Adriana: (sipping from the cup)
Hmm, this doesn't taste as boring as I thought it would. My husband has some unusual habits too, but unfortunately they're not healthy ones.

James:
Oh? Like what, for example?

Adriana: (looking annoyed)
Well, for a start, he's a real couch potato. Not that that's particularly unusual. Many men come home from work, flop down onto the sofa and then vegetate in front of the TV all evening. What's unusual is the type of junk food he eats while watching his videos.

James: (smiling)
Now I'm in suspense, Adriana. Tell me, what does he eat?

Adriana: (making a face)
Peanut butter and pickle sandwiches.

James: (laughing)
Oh, that's not so strange. I've tried that combination myself.

Adriana: (with a look of disbelief)
I can't believe it! You have?

James:
Sure, my mother is American, remember?
I know most Europeans think gastronomic culture in America is non-existent, but there really are many tasty, traditional dishes in addition to the infinite number of ethnic foods available in the States.

Unfortunately, worldwide, victims of American fast-food chains will forever picture the typical American with a hamburger in his hands.

Adriana: (gesturing with her hands)
Not to mention ketchup dripping out of the sides and a bottle of Coke nearby. I guess you're right. But peanut butter with pickles?

James: (imitating an American accent)
Yup. In this case, the pickles keep the peanut butter from sticking to the roof of your mouth.

Adriana tries to control her laughter as James continues.

James:
But what puzzles me, is how your husband ever got the idea of eating something so American in the land of pasta and pizza.

Adriana: (still smiling)
That's easy to explain. Antonio spent one year as an exchange student in a high school in Boston. He lived with a family that had two children his age and was introduced to every aspect of American life in the '60's.

James:
I'm sure that was a very enriching experience for him. And on that note, would you care for a chocolate-covered-raisin?

Adriana laughs as she moves forward to reach into the bag of chocolates James has extended towards her.
Regaining her composure, she continues to talk about Sun Club's public relations strategy and the trade fairs they will participate in.

Adriana: (pulling illustrations out of a folder)
Here are a few drawings of what our exhibit will look like and some samples of the brochures and leaflets we'll have printed.

James:
It all looks very professional. I like it.

Adriana: (glancing at her watch)
Oops! We had better be on our way now or we'll be late for our appointment.

They leave the office and arrive at the restaurant to find Mr. Gionelli already waiting for them at a table. As he rises and takes a step forward to greet them, his chic, tan leather shoes give a little squeak. Dressed in a stylish yet casual combination of trousers and a jacket, he looks as if he has just stepped out of the pages of a fashion magazine. After brief introductions are made, they order and then get down to business.

Mr. Gionelli: (pulling his chair closer)
In looking through the folder on your company's corporate identity, I believe we can make good use of your catchy slogan: "Fun in the Sun". It captures the audience's attention and lets them develop their own fantasies.

Adriana:
Yes, but please remember that we'll be addressing business people in this campaign. Our advertising must feature the additional facilities we now offer.

Mr. Gionelli: (looking optimistic)
I think your new product will be well-received. The concept is well-thought-out and you're already a market leader on the club resort scene. This means we won't have to start from scratch. Have you already decided how much of your budget will be allocated for advertising?

Adriana: (nodding)
Yes, we have. We're hoping to increase our turnover significantly with these new facilities, so we have sufficient funds at our disposal.

The lunch continues as Adriana gets more specific about the money Sun Club is willing to spend. After contributing his suggestions on celebrities to use for an endorsement, James sits back and listens to Adriana and Mr. Gionelli talk about the remaining details. The launch date of the campaign and the deadlines that have to be met are discussed. James feels confident that Adriana will make the right choice regarding which ad agency to use.

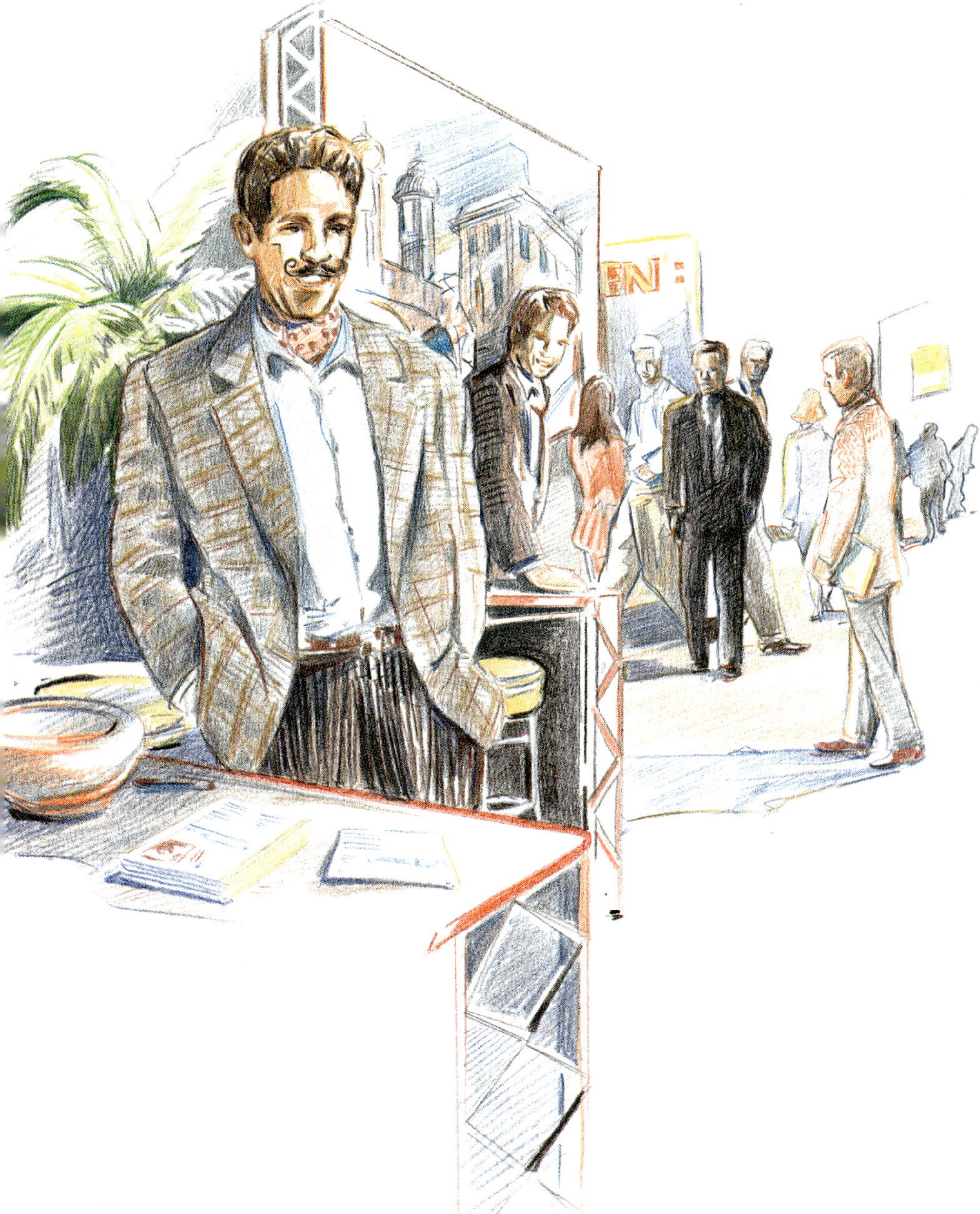

More than a year has passed since the corporate strategy meeting for the Virgin Islands project took place. Renovation and expansion of the former hotel complex has been completed and Otto Huber has taken over management of the newly opened U.S. Virgin Islands Sun Club.

Everyone is busy preparing for the club's first winter season. The marketing campaign is running smoothly and a travel trade fair is now taking place in Paris. As a part of Sun Club's sales promotion, Pierre Duclot, public relations expert and sales director of the Paris office, has invited travel agents of several European companies to attend a presentation on the club's new facilities. In order to get an impression of what's new on the market, James and Penny have also arrived in Paris to visit the travel fair and to attend Pierre's presentation. Pierre is waiting for them at Sun Club's stand. In his brown tweed jacket and corduroy pants, he could easily be mistaken for a British visitor. As he sees James and Penny walking over to one of Sun Club's displays, he quickly gives his handlebar moustache a little twist and fiddles with the silk scarf tied around his neck. Then he rushes over to them.

Pierre: (in a whisper)
James, Penny, how are you? Was it difficult to find the stand? How was the trip through the Chunnel? You look wonderful, Penny.

Giving Penny a little kiss on each cheek, he turns to shake James' hand.

James: (a bit surprised)
Please, Pierre, one question at a time. First of all, why are you whispering?

Pierre: (nervously wringing his hands)
Oh, it's awful, just awful! As you know, my presentation is scheduled for tomorrow evening, but I fear I'm losing my voice.
I've been so busy these past weeks, trying to organize everything for our exhibit. I've had a sore throat since yesterday and now I'm almost hoarse. What if I'm not able to speak tomorrow?

Penny: (in a sympathetic tone)
These halls are so drafty too. It's no wonder you've caught a cold. You're probably so run down that your body has no resistance to all the germs flying around here.

James: (clapping Pierre on the shoulder)
Don't worry, Pierre. If all else fails, I'll give your presentation. I'm sure it's well prepared and I don't mind delivering it.

Pierre: (looking relieved)
Would you really? It would be a great help. It's our kick-off presentation to set the ball rolling for the season, you know, and no one else in the office speaks English well enough to give this speech to our international guests. Oh, you've made my day!

James: (in a reassuring voice)
Sure, Pierre. It's really no problem. Let's wait and see how your voice sounds tomorrow morning.

Penny: (looking around)
The stand turned out very nicely, Pierre. Those eye-catching posters on that side-wall are very decorative.

Penny points to one side of the stand and then gestures with a nod of her head to where a large group of people have assembled.

Penny:
But I imagine the central attraction is the big screen over there where all the visitors are standing under the plastic palm trees.

Pierre: (eagerly nodding his head)
You're right. We had a very talented photographer put together a multi-media show on our clubs. We think a picture is worth a thousand words, so our sales reps are primarily here to answer questions and not to give a sales pitch.

James: (letting his eyes wander)
It looks as if there's an above-average turnout this year. The halls we came through were jam-packed. It took longer than we expected to get here.

Pierre:
Yes, supposedly four thousand people attended the opening ceremony this morning. Considering it was raining cats and dogs outside, that's an exceptional turnout.

As the three of them talk about the promotional events still scheduled to take place, Pierre's voice is slowly but surely getting worse. After advising him to rest his vocal cords, James and Penny agree to call him in the morning. They continue their walk through the endless, maze-like aisles of the travel fair.

Penny: (looking concerned)
Poor Pierre. He doesn't sound good at all.
He's usually such a talkative, sociable person.

James: (with a wry grin)
Yes, I've rarely seen him with his mouth shut so I'm sure it's difficult for him to suppress his dynamic personality.

Penny shoots him a look of disapproval as she tries to hold back a smile. Redirecting her attention to their surroundings, she politely declines the offers of exhibitors who try to lure her to their stands with promises of contests to be won to exotic, faraway places.
In the late afternoon, James and Penny take the Metro from the fair grounds back to their hotel. After resting a bit, they change their clothes for dinner and then meet in the lobby. As Penny approaches in a close-fitting, black velvet dress, James gives a little whistle of admiration.

James: (admiringly)
Penny, you take my breath away! Black looks positively elegant on you. It contrasts so beautifully with your red hair.

Penny: (looking pleased)
Thank you, James. The scarf you bought me in Spain for my birthday is just perfect for this dress. It really livens it up.

After James helps Penny into her coat, they step out of the hotel and James hails a cab. He takes her to a small, yet exclusive little restaurant he knows in the Latin Quarter.
An exquisitely-prepared candlelight dinner accompanied by classical guitar music begins to weave a spell of romance around them. Not wanting the evening to end, they stroll past the wrought-iron balconies of the narrow, winding streets, down to the Seine River. Arm in arm, they brave the cold, damp air as they walk along the left bank, past Notre Dame, gradually leaving the bohemian atmosphere of the Latin Quarter behind.

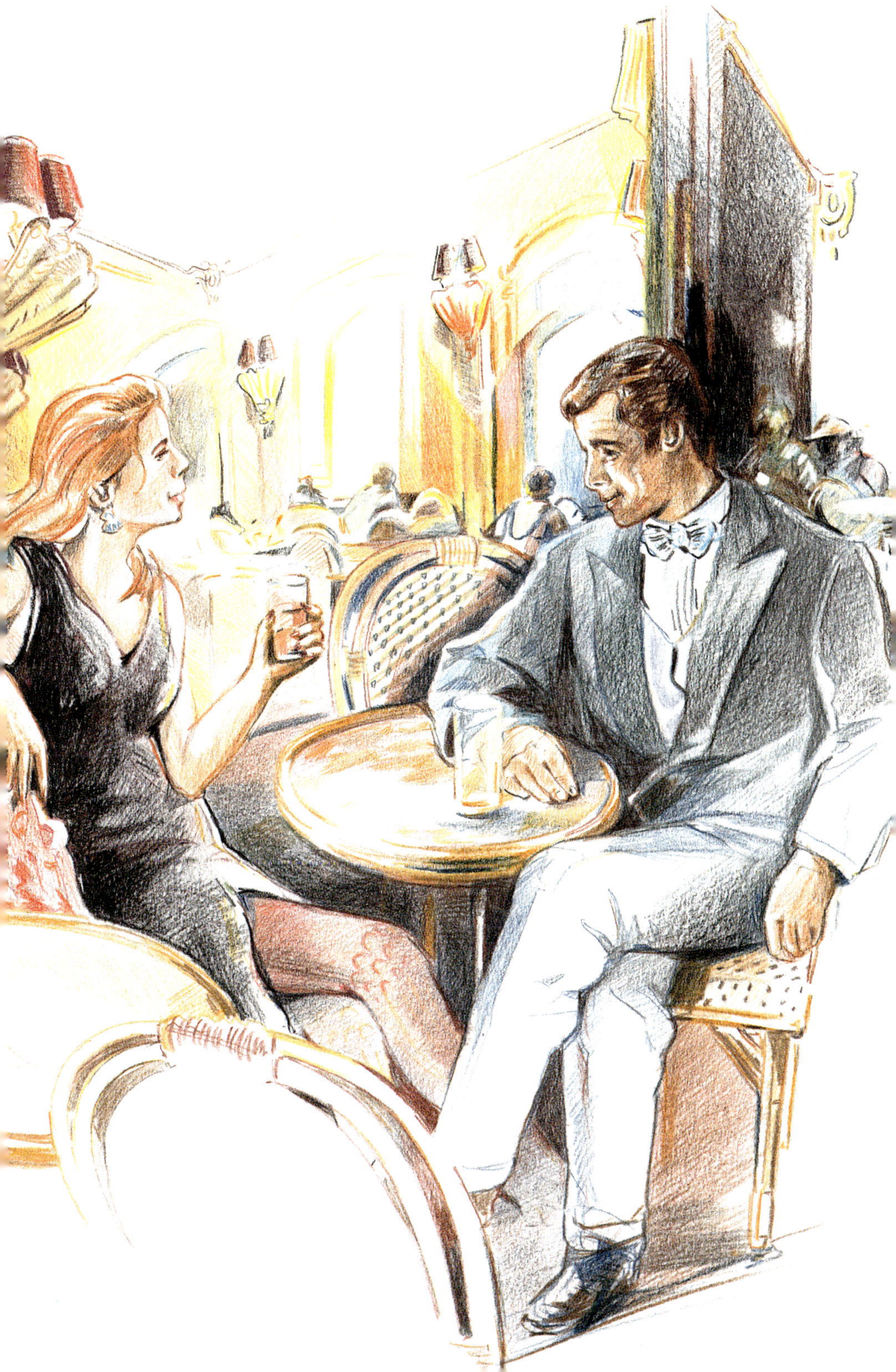

The next morning finds James in a terrible dilemma. Having suffered from a sudden case of diarrhea, the evening didn't end up quite as he had hoped. Weak and pale, he is now lying in bed with a slight temperature. What's even worse, Pierre has lost his voice completely. Neither of them is capable of giving the presentation. Hoping to find a solution to the problem, Pierre has joined Penny in James' hotel room.

Penny: (in her sympathetic voice)
Poor James. It began with a little upset stomach, but it must be something more serious. He didn't even ask for a chocolate-covered raisin this morning.

Pierre: (in a barely audible whisper)
It's probably the flu. You really look awful, James.

James: (frowning)
Thanks, same to you, Pierre. Now what do we do?

Penny looks from one dejected face to the other and then makes up her mind.

Penny: (with her hands on her hips)
Well, I guess there's really no choice. I'll have to give the presentation myself.

Both James' and Pierre's eyes widen as they stare at Penny.

Penny: (sounding cheerfully optimistic)
Don't worry boys. You've got all day to coach me on the delivery of this speech.
It should be a piece of cake.

James: (starting to get excited)
Now why didn't I think of that? Pierre, that's it! We've got all day to rehearse. They'll love her! Get out your speech! Sit over there! Penny, what would we do without you?

Quickly handing Penny some cue cards, Pierre pushes an armchair out of the way to set up a make-believe stage. Penny sits down to read through the short sentences of the text.

Pierre: (in a coarse whisper)
I'd like to begin by telling you something about your audience. Er, um...

Seeing that Pierre is having problems raising his voice, James quickly intervenes to give him a hand.

James:
Knowing exactly who you'll be speaking to will help to understand Pierre's objectives in planning the content of his presentation.

Pierre: (with a slight cough)
Um...right. Thanks. After a brief introduction to welcome our audience, we'll introduce the topic, outline the structure of our talk and cover the points we wish to make in a logical order.

Penny: (looking a little anxious)
What if I get nervous right at the beginning of the presentation?

Pierre:
I'll come back to this question later.

James: (consolingly)
Don't worry, Penny. Most people are nervous in such a situation. Just use the energy it gives you and remember to speak slowly and to make pauses. You establish rapport with your audience during the first few minutes and first impressions count.

Pierre: (nodding vigorously)
Right again. Actually, it might be best if you memorize the introduction. As for the conclusion: we'll briefly summarize the main points, thank the audience for their attention and invite questions.

James:
It's an old rule of thumb, Penny. "Tell them what you're going to tell them, tell them and then tell them what you told them."

Penny: (smiling)
Fine, but where do the visual aids come in?

Pierre: (reaching for his briefcase)
Okay, let's move on to this subject. I've decided against using diagrams, charts or graphs. A flipchart will be set up in one corner of the room and an overhead projector will be standing next to the podium for these transparencies.

Penny: (looking skeptical)
Wouldn't it be more effective to show a film clip from the multi-media show? Didn't you say a picture is worth a thousand words?

Pierre: (indecisive at first)
Hmm, you might be right. Now that you mention it, we could cut down your speaking time that way and many questions would probably answer themselves.

Penny: (still a bit insecure)
What if any hostile questions arise?

James:
We don't expect you to be 'under fire', but it's always good to be prepared. Just be your polite, diplomatic self, Penny. It's always been a good disarming tactic.

Penny's eyes twinkle and she has a mischievous grin on her face as she responds to James' teasing. The glances they exchange do not pass Pierre unnoticed. Clearing his throat, he tries to recapture their attention.

Pierre:
I'd like to summarize what I've said now.

As Pierre recaps the main points, James finishes up by giving Penny some additional tips on delivery. As she goes into the next room to practise, Pierre rests his voice and James, who is still not feeling well, excuses himself as he makes a dash for the bathroom.
Penny spends the rest of the afternoon rehearsing in front of the two sick men. Weak points in her speech are cleared up, her timing is improved and they manage to boost her confidence considerably. She looks enthusiastic about her subject matter, maintains good eye contact and varies the intonation of her voice on a regular basis.
By the end of the afternoon, all three of them are convinced that she will give an excellent presentation. This time Penny has come to the rescue.

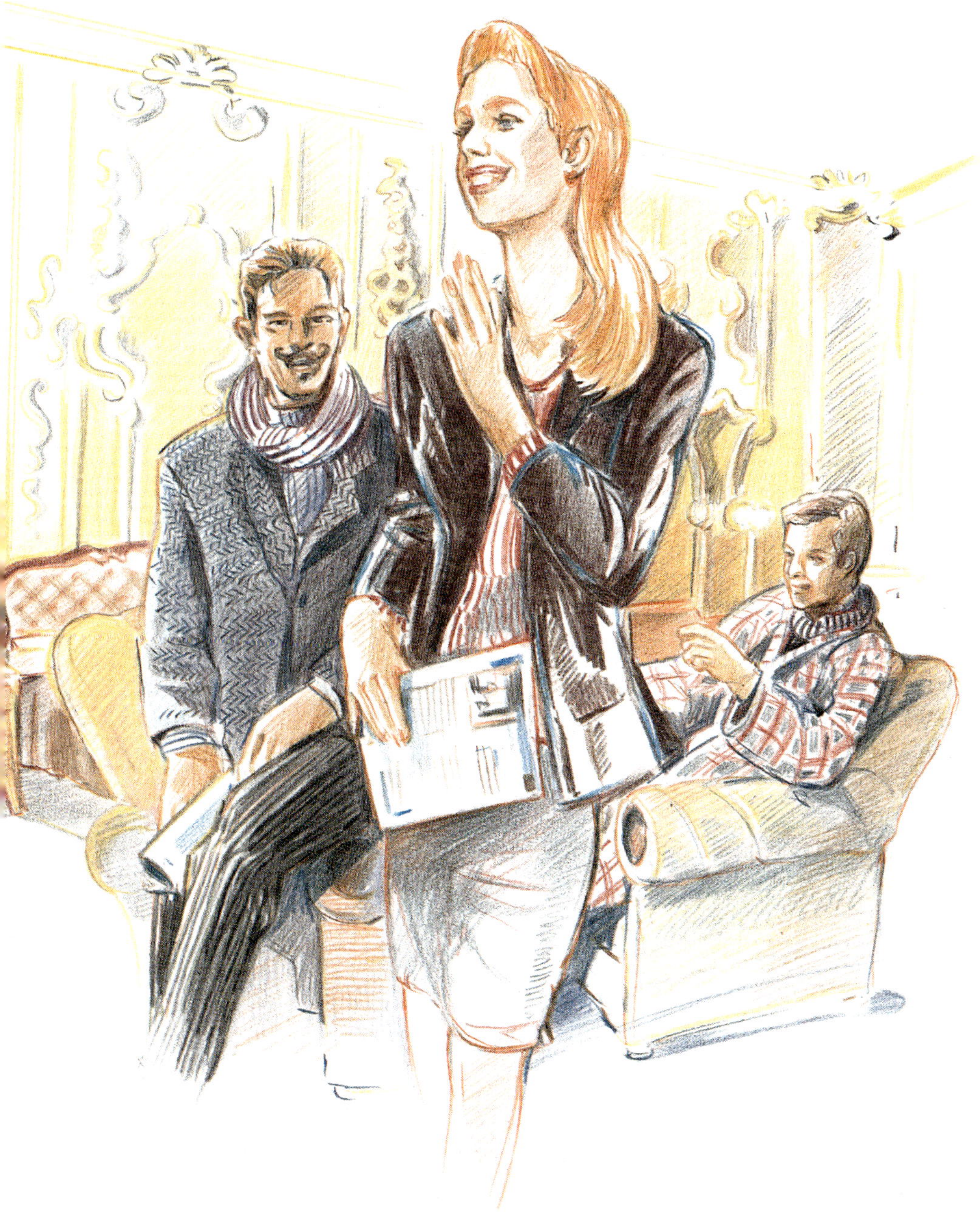

8

*T*he first winter season has turned out to be a great success for Sun Club's newest resort. Everyone who has worked on the project is glad that their efforts have paid off. Yet it's James' and Penny's job to find out how the club can be improved still further.

With the help of the customer service department, all of the comments and suggestions for improvement made by the club's guests have been evaluated. The results of the evaluation show that there are some weak spots in the entertainment program.

A few letters of complaint have been forwarded to Jannie Van Vliet, the entertainment expert and sales director of the Netherlands branch office. James has received selected copies of these letters and has decided to visit Jannie in Amsterdam.

They are now sitting in her office at a round table made of light-colored pine. Surrounded by antique furniture and several large plants, the room has a cozy atmosphere.

Jannie is a small, fun-loving 29-year-old woman. With her extremely short, white-blond hair, flowery-patterned pants outfit and spontaneous personality, she's like a splash of color in the room. Although she is sensitive and emotional about the letters, she is a professional and takes the complaints very seriously.

Jannie:
I must admit, I thrive on stress, but this thing has me off balance and seems to be draining my energy.

James:
Well, stress is more than just a popular word in today's world, Jannie. It's a part of everyday life and a lot of research is being done on it. The expression "eustress" has been coined for the positive, challenging kind of stress you say you thrive on. But what you're facing now is probably "distress", the negative kind that can wear you out.

Jannie: (sighing)
Gee, I'm glad I don't have to face distress very often. My work environment is pleasant. I make sure my job stays varied and interesting and I'm not a workaholic. But this matter is something I can't delegate.
As outspoken as I am, I'm absolutely tongue-tied when it comes to responding to a complaint.

James: (smiling)
That's not unusual, Jannie.
Most people take any kind of criticism very personally and get too emotional when they respond.

Jannie: (exasperated)
You're right.
I got pretty upset reading these letters, but at least when I respond to something written, I have time to think about it. What's really difficult, is when I'm put on the spot in person or on the phone.

James:
Well, first of all, it's important to give the person who has a complaint enough uninterrupted time to get everything he wants to say off his chest. Allowing him to blow off steam usually has a calming effect.
The second step is to recognize and acknowledge that this person has a valid reason for being unhappy about something. Even if you don't think it's valid, he does.
This isn't an admission of guilt or doesn't imply that we were at fault in any way. It simply shows sympathy and can lead to a joint problem-solving attitude: "We have a problem. Let's see how we can solve it."

Jannie: (listening attentively)
But what if I need more time to react because I still don't know what to say?

James:
You can gain time and work wonders using expressions like "Really?" or "Can you give me a few more details about this, please?" A question like: "Could you just say that slowly, so I can make a note of it, please?" will even demonstrate how concerned you are about getting the facts straight.

Jannie: (pondering what has been said)
Hmm. I think I get your point. It certainly gives me something new to work with.

James:
What exactly happened with this group of businessmen and their wives who were staying at our club in February?

Jannie: (spreading the file out on the table)
Well, it seems their travel agent misled them into believing the famous magician we've been using in our ads is a regular part of our entertainment program.
They actually expected to see him performing in our club and were very disappointed when he didn't show up.

James:
Have you spoken to the travel agency yet?

Jannie: (shaking her head)
No. That was going to be my next step after talking to you. I think this tour operator has been doing some false advertising.

James: (looking concerned)
That would be a very serious charge, Jannie. I sincerely hope it's just a simple misunderstanding.

Jannie:
So do I. I wouldn't want to have to threaten them with legal action. This is the second time we've received a complaint from a group booked through them.

James: (reaching for the file)
Jannie, do you mind if I make the call to the tour operator?

Jannie: (gesturing toward the phone)
No, not at all. I'd love to see how you handle this.

Jannie presses the phone's loudspeaker button to listen in on the call as James dials the number she has given him. After a few rings, a pre-recorded message on the company's answering machine can be heard.

"You have reached Gulliver's Travels. We're sorry, but all our agents are busy right now. Please hold the line or try again in a few minutes."

James: (hanging up the phone)
Well, that didn't get us very far. Do you mind if I give Penny a quick call before I try again?

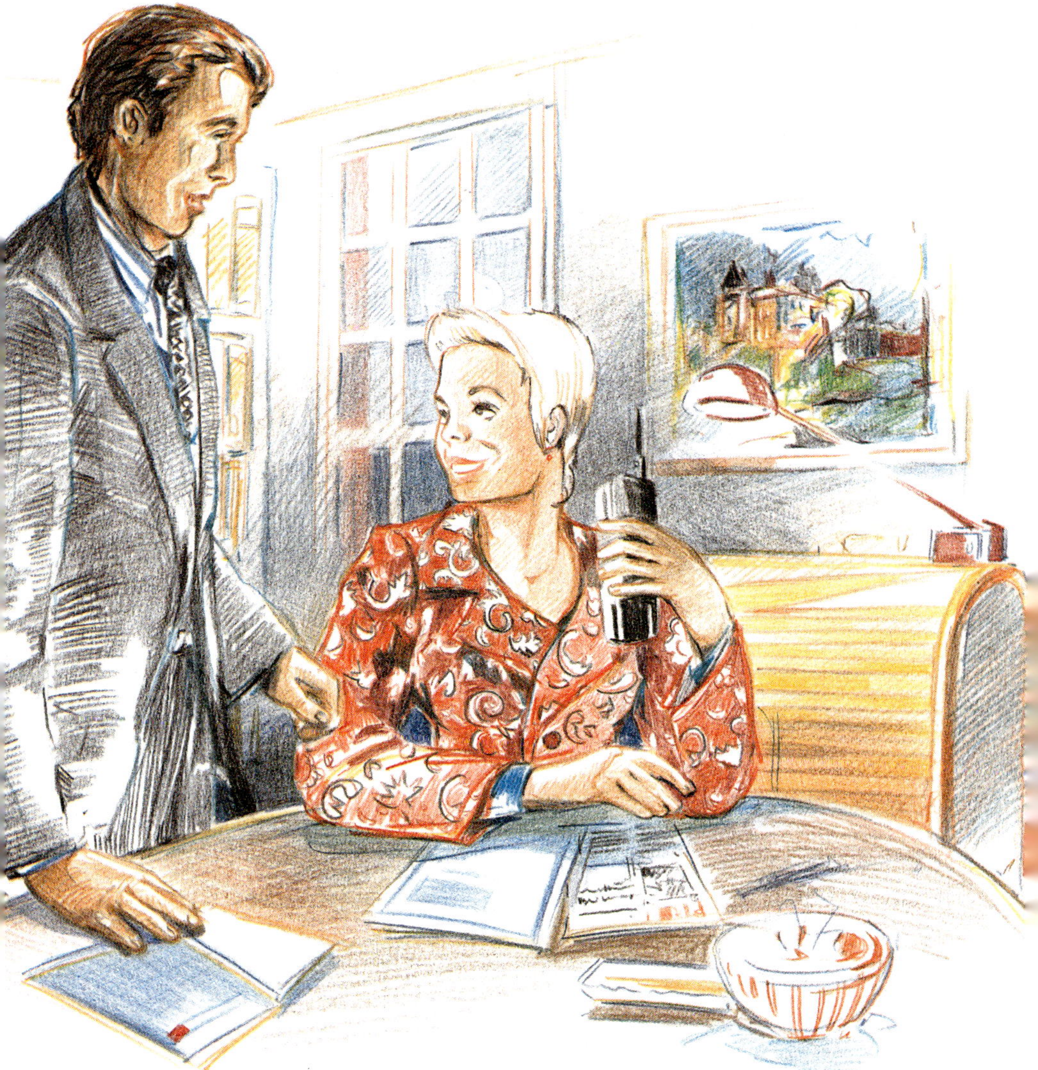

Jannie: (getting up from her chair)
Sure, go ahead. In the meantime, I'll get us some coffee... or do you still prefer plain hot water?

James: (nodding)
Yes, I do. Thanks, Jannie.

As Jannie walks out the door, James dials the country code for England in order to make the long distance call. After a few rings, James recognizes Penny's pleasant voice, despite the static in the background.

Penny:
Sun International, Penny McCloud speaking.

James: (speaking loudly)
Hi Penny, it's me. Any messages?

Penny: (faintly)
Oh, James, I was just going to call you. You won't believe what's happened! Otto Huber's father has passed away. It was very sudden, a heart attack, I believe. In any case, Mr. Wadsworth would like to speak to you right away. Shall I connect you?

James:
No, Penny. It's a very bad line. Can you have him call me back at Jannie's extension, here in Amsterdam?

Penny agrees and they exchange a few words of concern for how Otto must be feeling before James hangs up. A few moments later, the phone rings. James lifts the receiver.

James:
James Thorne speaking.

Mr. Wadsworth's secretary:
James? This is Nancy. Just a moment, please. I'll put you through to Mr. Wadsworth.

Jonathan:

James, how are you? Sorry to disturb you out there in Amsterdam, but this matter couldn't wait. Otto says he has to leave us!
He regrets it, of course, but says he must take over his parents´ ski hotel in the Alps. How on earth are we going to get a new general manager on such short notice?

James: (speaking slowly)
Well, this is all very sudden. Give me a few minutes to think about it, Jonathan.

Happy to have received a little hint from Penny, Jonathan waits in anticipation of what James will say next.

James: (hesitantly)
Well, you know, I think I'm ready for a change. This might seem a little impetuous, but would you consider putting me in charge of the Virgin Islands Club?

Jonathan: (enthusiastic)
James, I was hoping you'd say that! Nobody knows the new place better than you do.
You've got my blessing, as long as I can call on you every now and then, when trouble arises.

James: (surprised but pleased)
Why, of course, Jonathan. I appreciate that. You know you can count on me.

They talk briefly about the details involved in taking over the club. The conversation ends just as Jannie enters the room carrying a tray with two cups and a bowl of mixed nuts with raisins.

Jannie: (setting down the tray)
Sorry. No chocolate in the house, James. This is the best I can offer you.

James: (looking proud of himself)
Oh, didn't you know? I've given up chocolate. I just quit from one day to the next. It certainly impressed Penny. I don't mind if I have some raisins though.

As one hand pops a raisin into his mouth, the other lifts up the receiver to call the tour operator again. This time a live voice answers.

Travel agent:
Gulliver's Travels. Wilma Rijkers speaking.

James:
Hello, I'd like to speak to the manager of your company, please.

Travel agent:
Oh, I'm afraid he's rather tied up at the moment. May I ask who's calling, please?

James:
This is James Thorne of the Sun Club division of Sun International calling from our Amsterdam office.

Travel agent: (taking a note pad)
Would you like to leave a message? I could ask Mr. Hoofddorp to call you back.

James:
Yes, please ask him to call me back as soon as possible. My number here is 599-3260.

Travel agent:
I'm sorry. I didn't catch that completely. Could you please repeat the last two numbers? Oh, just a moment... here comes Mr. Hoofddorp now. Please hold on while I connect you, Mr. Thorne.

After a brief interlude of relaxing music, a deep voice answers.

Mr. Hoofddorp:
Max Hoofddorp. How can I help you?

James:
Mr. Hoofddorp, My name is Thorne, James Thorne. I'm calling on behalf of Sun International's Sun Club division.

James proceeds by explaining the problem as Mr. Hoofddorp listens patiently. He seems to be familiar with the incident and knows which agent has created the mix-up.

Mr. Hoofddorp: (in a conciliatory voice)
Please accept our sincere apologies for the inconvenience this has caused. The agent who booked these groups was hired by us on a commission basis to help out during our peak season. He's no longer with us, but unfortunately, the damage has already been done. We'll take the necessary steps to ensure that such a mistake doesn't occur again.

James:
We trust you'll also be getting in touch with the groups involved, to explain what happened.

Mr. Hoofddorp:
Yes, naturally we will send a letter of apology to both groups. We have many companies interested in your clubs and we are anxious to settle this matter to everyone's complete satisfaction.

Appeased, both James and Jannie are satisfied with the results of the phone call. To show that Sun Club has taken action, Jannie decides that she will also send an official response to the complaint. This, she hopes, will settle the matter once and for all.
After a fun evening out with Jannie discussing how the entertainment program might still be improved, James is back in his hotel room reclining on the bed. Although it's relatively late, he reaches over to the phone resting on the nightstand and dials Penny's home number.

Penny: (in a sleepy voice)
Hello?

James:
It's me, James. I'm sorry, did I wake you up?

Penny: (reaching for her alarm clock)
Don't worry. I had only just fallen asleep. But James, it's almost midnight. What's up?

James:
Well, I'm sorry we couldn't talk longer on the phone today. This business with Otto has really got me thinking.

Penny: (sensing something)
Yes, poor Otto. I really feel sorry for him. He enjoyed living on St. John very much. I'm sure he'll miss the club and the magnificent sunsets.

James: (tentatively)
Well, actually, that's kind of what I'm calling about. I've agreed to take over management of the Virgin Islands Club.

Penny: (excited)
Oh, James! Really?! That's wonderful!

James: (searching for words)
Yeah, and... well, Penny... I'd really like you to come with me. Remember when we were daydreaming about lying on the beach last year. It's been on my mind a lot since then.
Why don't we get out of the rat-race in Europe and start a new life together on the islands? What do you say, Penny?

The pause is filled with silence as James holds his breath.

Penny:
James, I'd love to!

James: (with a breath of relief)
Oh Penny, what would I do without you?

CORPORATE STRATEGY/MEETING PEOPLE

The following symbols will be used in the skills section of each unit:

- is for written practice
- is for listening comprehension and verbal training
- lets you know that you need your cassette recorder / CD player
- tells you the following text can only be heard (a transcript is included in the index)

INTRODUCTIONS

> "**How do you do**" is a greeting, not a question.
> So don't tell people about your indigestion.

There are many ways to introduce yourself or others in English: depending on the situation, it can be formal or informal. Here are a few examples of the introductions at Sun Club:

Formal: Ms. Saladino, *may I introduce you to* Mr. Thorne?
Mr. Thorne, Ms. Saladino.
(women or older persons are introduced first.)

How do you do. My name is Adriana Saladino.
Pleased to meet you. Please call me James.

Jannie, *I'd like you to meet* Pierre. Pierre *this is* Jannie.
Pleased to meet you.
The pleasure is mine.

Informal: Penny, *have you met* Fritz? Fritz *this is* Penny.
Nice to meet you. Likewise.
Hello. (British) Hi. (US)

SKILLS 84

Don't be a wallflower.
Introduce yourself.

Imagine you are at Sun Club and want to introduce yourself:

Excuse me, I don't think we've met. My name is ...

Introductions are easy when you realize there are many varieties to choose from. Just pick one you feel comfortable with and then experiment. Remember: You can say "How do you do" in response to a greeting of "How do you do".

EXERCISE 1-1 WHAT NATIONALITY ARE THEY?

Like most business people in Europe, at one time or another you will come into contact with other nationalities. It's good to be familiar with the terms used for the country, language and inhabitants (*people*). Here are the participants of our meeting at Sun Club. What nationality are they and what language do they speak?

Jannie is from **The Netherlands** (or Holland) and is _____(a). Fritz is from **Germany** and is _____(b). Pierre comes from **France** and is _____(c). Adriana is from **Italy** and is _____(d). José is from **Spain** and is _____(e). Penny is from **Scotland** and is _____(f). Jonathan is from **England** and is _____(g). (Penny and Jonathan can also be called British or Brits for short) James' mother is from America and is _____(h).

SKILLS

Sometimes in English we have another word for the inhabitants of a country that is slightly different from the one used for the country and the language. For example, José is from **Spain**, speaks **Spanish**, eats **Spanish** paella and his people are called **the Spaniards**. See if you recognize some others:

1. Denmark: Carlsberg is a _____ beer. The _____ like to drink it.

2. Sweden: IKEA is a _____ furniture company. The _____ buy a lot of it.

3. Finland: Helsinki is a _____ city. The _____ are very good at designing.

4. Turkey: You can drink _____ coffee in Istanbul. The _____ drink it often.

5. Poland: You can buy _____ sausages in Poland. The _____ like to eat them.

SOCIALIZING: Chit chat and all that

When you meet people for the first time, it's nice to find that you have something in common. Think about the things you find interesting and easy to talk about. The next time you meet colleagues from other countries you can try them out. You can ask about hobbies and interests:

| What | sort
kind
type | of | books
films
music
sport | do you like? | | I love
I enjoy

I like
I don't mind

I don't like
I hate |

SKILLS 86

You can find out how often they do something:

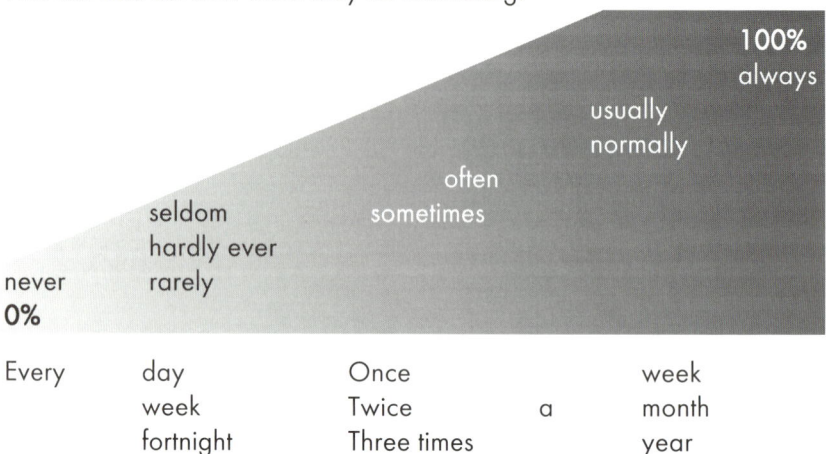

```
                                          100%
                                          always
                                usually
                                normally
                        often
        seldom          sometimes
        hardly ever
never   rarely
0%
```

Every	day	Once		week
	week	Twice	a	month
	fortnight	Three times		year

EXERCISE 1-2 IN THE CAR

James is picking up José at the airport the evening before the meeting. Listen on your cassette/CD to the dialogue as James drives José to his hotel: Imagine you are welcoming James as a visitor to your home town. How do you think the conversation might go? Have fun!

James, nice to see you again. Is this your first time in _____?

Yes, _____. I'd love to see

_____.

Would you like me to show you around after the meeting?

Yes, that's very _____. Is there a good

_____?

Yes, there is. Are you interested in _____?

Yes. I play _____ and I _____. What about you?

I _____.

SKILLS

Now we have everyone arriving for the meeting. But what happened first to bring them to London? Yes, you're right, Jonathan sent everyone a memorandum (*memo*) to inform them of the meeting. In the memo Jonathan gave the following information:

date the memo is written
sender's name and **position** in the company
the **person and/or position** the memo is sent to
the **subject** briefly explains what the memo is about
the **agenda** covers the purpose of the meeting

Here is the memo each of the Sales Directors received: (most companies have specially printed forms)

MEMORANDUM

SUN INTERNATIONAL

Date: Sept. 19, 19..
From: Jonathan Wadsworth, Senior Exec. VP
To: European Sales Directors
Subject: Virgin Islands project

The meeting will be held on Tuesday, October 4th, at 9 a.m. in the London office.

It is imperative that all European sales directors are present.

AGENDA

> We will discuss the corporate strategy for our new club resort in the Virgin Islands. This is the first time conference facilities will be offered and your expertise is required. Please bring a list of strategic objectives within your field.

Thank you.

SKILLS

There are a number of questions to be answered, such as:

Who is going to attend the meeting? (*persons*)
What is on the agenda? (*topic or subject*)
Why is the meeting taking place? *(reason)*
When will it take place? (*time*)
Where will it take place? (*place*)
How shall we proceed? (*procedure*)

Using "**do**" as a helping verb to ask specific questions:

Do you know **who** was at the meeting?
Yes, **I do**. No, **I don't**.
Do we know **where** the meeting was held?
Yes, we **do**. No, we **don't**.
Do they know **what** was discussed at the meeting?
Does Penny know **why** they had a meeting?
Yes, she **does**. No, she **doesn't**.
Does Fritz know **when** the meeting took place?
Does the secretary know **how** everyone arrived for the meeting?

EXERCISE 1-3 TAKING THE MINUTES

There are several ways to record what was discussed at a meeting. The **minutes** are an **official record** of these discussions and the decisions made at a meeting. Since you also attended the meeting at Sun Club you offer to help Penny finish typing the minutes because her laptop battery is weak and some important words are missing. Fill in the missing words from the list on the right and help her finish on time!

MINUTES OF THE MANAGEMENT MEETING

Held at ____ _____ of Sun International on Tuesday, October 4th, at 9 a.m.

Present: J. Wadsworth, J. Thorne, F. Fischer, A. Saladino, P. Duclot, J. Aquilar, J. Van Vliet, P. McCloud (took the minutes).

_____ of the last meeting

The minutes of the last meeting were _____, taken as read and signed as a true _____

Matters arising

_____ strategy for building a new club _____ in the Virgin Islands.

First time that Sun Club will offer conference _____.

Discussion

Brainstorming of all concerned for ideas to _____ in _____ strategy.

Summary

It was _____ that the following _____ are important:

1. Identify greatest _____ and make use of them
2. Be unique
3. Be _____
4. Cooperate instead of _____ with the competition
5. Think _____ group rather than product-oriented
6. Concentrate on the _____ not variable needs of customer
7. Be quick to change

Meeting _____ at 12:30 p.m. Next meeting _____ for November 6th when _____ directors report findings.

---

sales
criteria
circulated
scheduled
record
facilities
resolved
overall
competing
head
office
target
adjourned
resort
strengths
corporate
minutes
consider
innovative
basic

SKILLS

All work and no play makes for a dull day. So, let's go with the rest of the Sun Club employees to a local restaurant to eat. I hope you're hungry! Have a look first at the menu of the specialties being offered and then listen to your cassette/CD to the conversation in the restaurant:

EXERCISE 1-4 IN THE RESTAURANT

BUSINESS LUNCH MENU

STARTERS
Partan Bree
rich Scottish crab soup with garlic bread
Quail's Eggs
in haddock and cheese sauce
Cock-a-Leekie
chicken, leek and barley soup

MAIN COURSE
Roast Beef
served with Yorkshire Pudding
Dover Sole
poached and served in a sorrel sauce
Roast Leg of Welsh Lamb
served with mint sauce

SWEETS
Spotted Dick
A classic bread and butter pudding with raisins
Strawberries and Cream
fresh strawberries and cream
Chocolate Fudge Cake
a rich, sticky chocolate cake
Cheese
A wide selection of British cheeses

JOKE: Customer: *"Waiter, there's a dead fly in my wine."*
Waiter: *"Well, you did order a wine with a little body in it, didn't you?"*

SKILLS

TIPPING: Before ordering in Britain, check the small print at the bottom of the menu. Prices should include VAT (Value Added Tax) but not necessarily service (between 10 and 15%). Beware of the old trick where service is included in the bill but staff leave the "total" box on your credit slip blank, hoping you will add another 10%. In America a 15-20% tip is standard (service is not included) and most people simply double the sales tax.

Penny collects various "words of wisdom" and sayings. Murphy's Laws by A. Bloch are some of her favorites. Like this one:

> **Murphy's Law**
> *Everybody should believe in something - I believe I'll have another drink.*

How would you describe your country's specialties to a visitor? Here are a few suggestions to help you:

- It's a popular local speciality.
- It's (a little) like ...
- It's sour.
- It's a vegetable (meat, etc.)
- It's marinated in ...
- It's very rich.
- It's a seasonal dish.
- It's a bit salty.
- They're cooked with ...
- It's made with ...
- It's sweet
- It's sour. It's spicy (hot).
- It has a strong flavor.
- It's a type of ...

Adriana and José are the newcomers in Sun Club, but it isn't often that the opportunity arises for all of the major sales directors to meet at the same time. To take advantage of the situation, Penny has arranged a little party in the evening so that everyone from the meeting can become better acquainted and meet the other members of the staff in London. Everyone is having a ball (*a lot of fun*) as you can see!

I'm terribly sorry. 1
You're Portuguese aren't you? 2
I didn't catch your name. 3
Would you like to visit Rome? 4
Do try these canapes. 5
How's business? 6
Cheers! 7
Would you like a drink? 8
I'm afraid there's no more Port. 9
Let me give you a lift back to your hotel. 10
This is Justin Browne. 11
Have you met Pierre? 12

SKILLS

EXERCISE 1-5 AT A PARTY!

Now match the reply given below to the question or comment in the picture opposite. Have fun!

a) Thanks. They look delicious.
b) No, I'm Spanish.
c) Yes please. I'll have a gin . tonic water.
d) Well, then I'll have a sherry . instead
e) How do you do.
f) No I haven´t. Nice to meet you.
g) It's Jennifer. Jennifer Alexander.
h) That's very nice of you but I'd like to walk.
i) Don't worry. It's only
j) Not bad, and how's life treating you?
k) Cheers!
l) Yes, I'd love to.

a.) - 5

b.)

SKILLS
NEGOTIATIONS

It's Saturday morning and James has picked Mr. Garfield up at his hotel. They've decided to play some golf with Jonathan who is already waiting for them at the golf course. If you don't already play the game, here's a chance to familiarize yourself with some golf terminology.

EXERCISE 2-1 FORE!

After reading the transcript, see if you can match the golfing terms with their correct definition:

1. **par**
2. **handicap**
3. **tee off**
4. **driving range**
5. **fairway or green**
6. **putting green**

a. an area used for practising long shots in golf
b. the standard number of strokes needed to hit the ball into the hole
c. the well-groomed, grassy area
d. the number of additional strokes above par needed to hit the ball into the hole
e. a small lawn area used to practise putting the ball into the hole from a short distance
f. starting the game by hitting the ball off the first tee

SKILLS
Useful Phrases for Meetings

Now that you're feeling confident in social situations, let's move on to some useful phrases appropriate for meetings. In Unit 2 Mr. Garfield arrives on Friday, plays several rounds of golf with Jonathan and James over the weekend and begins negotiations with them on Monday morning. In the following examples taken from the text, find the lead-in phrase from the list. Any selection from each grouping could be correct depending on the situation and you may find many of these expressions useful in **your** next meeting.

EXERCISE 2-2 AT A MEETING

STARTING A MEETING

Shall we get started?
We need to discuss ...
Our objective today ...
Let's begin now, shall we ...

Jonathan:
___ _____ _____
should be ...

AGREEING

Strong:
Absolutely! Precisely! Exactly!
That goes without saying!
I fully/quite/totally agree

Bill:
_ _____ _____ , plus
any additional supplies ...

Neutral:
That's true.
I agree.
That's correct.
I think you're right.

Jonathan:
_____ _____. It
would greatly reduce our ...

Bill:
_ _____ ____ _____ . I'd like to
make the most out of my property ...

Not so sure:
Maybe you're right.
I suppose so.
I tend to agree.
Perhaps.

Bill:
Well, _____ ____ _____ . I tend to
get too personally involved ...

SKILLS   96
DISAGREEING

Strong:
Definitely not! Nonsense!
Of course not.
That's out of the question.
I totally disagree.
Neutral:
I'm afraid I don't agree.
I don't really think so.
I can't quite agree with you.
Not so sure:
I'm not so sure.
So you really think so?
Is that such a good idea?

Jonathan:
___ _____ I _____ _____ with you there. Dependent upon our ...

Bill:
_____ ___ __ ___ _____! I've been running a family business here.

Bill:
Mmmm, ___ ___ __ ____ . I'm not quite convinced yet.

MAKING A SUGGESTION

I suggest ...
My suggestion would be ...
Nevertheless we could ...
In addition to ... we could ...
Perhaps we should ...
What about ... ?
It might be worth ...
Why don't we ...

James:
_ _____ we put Sun Club personnel in some key management positions, ...

James:
_____ , __ _____ help make you a very happy pensioner some day.

CHECKING COMPREHENSION

Does that mean ... ?
So what you're saying is ...
What exactly do you mean?
To put that another way ...
In other words ...

Bill:
__ ____ _____ _____ __ that some people will get the "golden parachute" ...

SKILLS
GIVING AN OPINION

Strong:
I have no doubt ...
I'm convinced ...
I'm quite sure that ...
Neutral:
It appears to me ...
I think ...
As I/ we see it ...
In my opinion ...
Not so sure:
It seems to me ...
Well, I tend to think ...
I feel ...
It looks as if ...

James:
__ __ _____ , getting personally involved is more of an advantage ...

Bill:
__ ____ __ _____ that using local raw materials, ... will keep production costs at a minimum.

EXPRESSING DOUBTS

Maybe that's true, but ...
I suppose you're right, but ...
You have a point, ...
I'm not sure if ...
I doubt that, but ...

Jonathan:
___ ____ _ _____ , but although we discussed taking over ...

COMING BACK TO THE MAIN POINT

I think we're getting side-tracked.
Let's move on to ...
Could we get back to ... ?

Jonathan:
Now _____ ____ __ __ some essential questions Penny still has open.

SUMMING UP

So, we all agree?
Let's briefly review ...
We are going to ...

Penny sums up the main points before they adjourn.

Good luck in **your** next meeting!

Sign in a company:

> In our company all colleagues are equal - only the salaries aren't.

The *joint venture* or *alliance* that Mr. Garfield and Sun Club discuss during their meeting is one way that companies can try to strengthen their operations, increase profits or stay competitive. There are two other ways: a *merger* or an *acquisition* (also known as a *takeover*).

IT´S A DEAL!

Joint Venture or Alliance: This term is used for a company formed jointly by two or more companies. It can also refer to a partnership that is usually temporary, but can sometimes become permanent, between two or more companies for a special business activity. The partners share the costs and profits in agreed proportions.

Merger: This is when two companies, often about the same size or in the same industry, combine to form one new company in order to increase their market share, to be more competitive and to cut costs in areas such as research and development. Another form of merger is when one company, usually the larger one, obtains ownership of the other company which then becomes a subsidiary, and may or may not keep it's name. A **shotgun merger** is a merger forced by one company on another that does not have the financial means to stop it.

Acquisition or Takeover: This is when one company offers the shareholders of another company what is called a takeover bid; i.e. (*that means*) an offer to buy the shares needed for a controlling interest in the company at a price higher than the market value. If the shareholders agree, the company can take over control and ownership. A **hostile takeover** is made without the agreement and against the wishes of the company being taken over. A **creeping takeover** is when shares of a company are bought slowly and quietly from individual shareholders until there are enough to take control.

SKILLS

Last year Penny went on holiday to the Greek island of Naxos and found the following on the wall of a romantic tavern:

TO BE IS TO DO	TO DO IS TO BE	DO BE DO BE DO
Socrates	Sartre	Sinatra

When James suggests putting Sun Club personnel in key management positions, Bill asks if some of his employees will get the *"golden parachute"*. Using a form of the word "gold" (which most people associate with wealth), has become increasingly popular in the business world. According to the "Oxford Dictionary of New Words", a golden parachute is a sum of money paid to an executive as compensation for losing their job, often because a company changes hands. Similar sums paid to lower-ranking employees are called "tin parachutes".

GO FOR GOLD!

Here are some more visual expressions using the word "golden":

Golden Handshake: a sum of money paid to an employee when they retire or are made redundant.

Golden Handcuffs: these are benefits provided by the employer that make it difficult or unattractive for the employee to work anywhere else.

Golden Hello: a big lump sum of money, over and above salary, offered by a prospective employer to induce an executive to accept a job.

Golden Retriever: a sum of money paid to someone who has already left a company to persuade them to return.

Golden Bullet: In marketing this term is used for a product that is extremely successful.

Golden Share: A controlling interest in a company, especially one that has recently been privatized, allowing the **Golden Shareholder** (usually the government) to veto policies they don't like.

SKILLS
PHRASAL VERBS

In modern English we often use a combination of a verb with a preposition or an adverb. It can be confusing to see one verb with many different meanings. The important thing to **keep in mind** (*remember*) is to consider the expression as a whole. It could be an idiom or part of one. You will find some of these phrasal verbs used in each unit. Take a *look at* the following examples:

to look at	James, Bill and Jonathan **look at** Penny's flaming red hair.
to look back	First, they **looked back** at what was discussed in the Virgin Islands last month.
to look for	Sun Club **was looking for** a partner.
to look forward to	Mr. Garfield **has been looking forward to** meeting Penny.
to look into	They **will have to look into** the costs of upgrading the existing structures.
to look through	Penny **has looked through** the tax statements that Bill brought with him.
to look s.o. up	Next time James is in Rome he **is going to look up** Adriana.
to look up s.th.	If you had a good dictionary you **would look up** many words.

EXERCISE 2-3 MATCH THEM UP

Now match up the definitions with the correct form of *"to look"*:

1. expect with pleasure
2. consider the past
3. visit someone
4. search for
5. examine things
6. regard s.th. or s.o.
7. find information
8. investigate

a) to look at
b) to look back
c) to look for
d) to look forward to
e) to look into
f) to look through
g) to look s.th. up
h) to look s.o. up

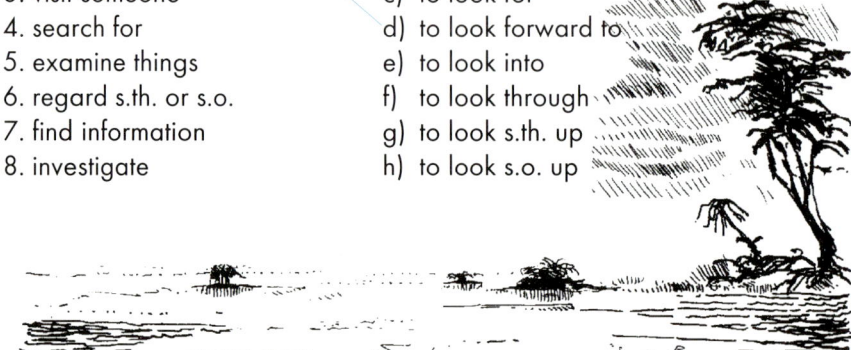

101 SKILLS

EXERCISE 2-4 FILL IN THE SQUARES

James is a big fan of crossword puzzles. Are you? Using the key word "preliminary talks" down as a guide, complete the puzzle using the definitions below. Have fun!

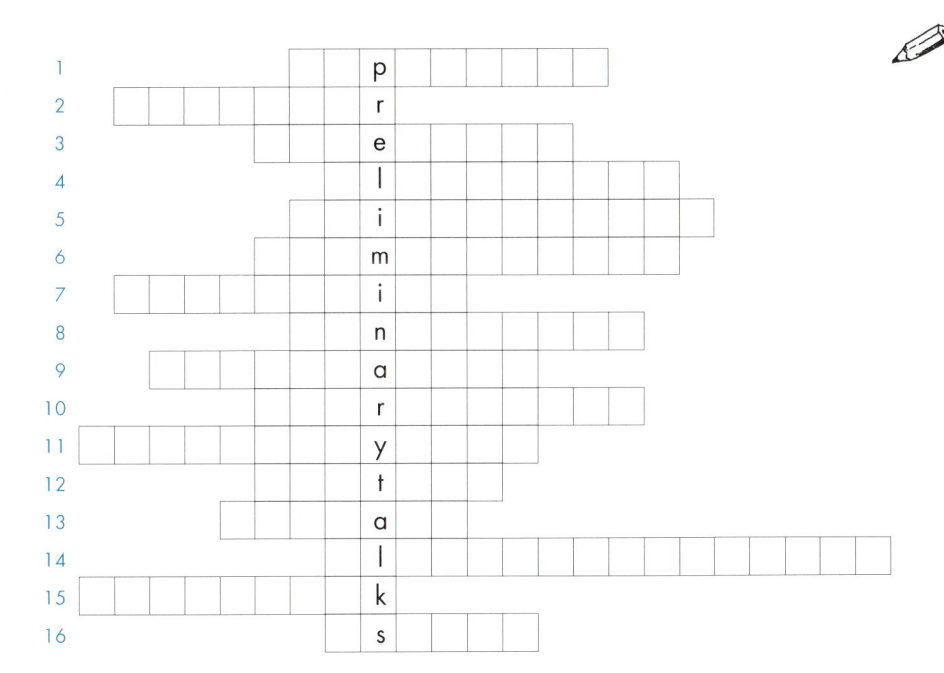

Across:
1. when something is made larger than it is now
2. person who buys shares or property
3. process of digesting food
4. drawings of building plans
5. partnership between two companies (*two words*)
6. the base used to manufacture something (*two words*)
7. official persons in power, official organization
8. when you fix up a building or modernize it
9. a discussion held to reach an agreement
10. when something loses its value, it ...
11. a list of goods or furniture (*two words*)
12. too much paperwork from authorities
13. to raise to a higher quality
14. a letter to say what you plan to do (*four words*)
15. manufacturer's name or emblem
16. property with a monetary value

SKILLS 102

Penny and James have had two successful meetings because they were well-prepared. Thanks to Penny's efficiency and James' diplomacy, everything is moving along faster than expected and Mr. Garfield has returned to the Virgin Islands with a good feeling about the upcoming venture.

EXERCISE 2-5 CULTURAL AWARENESS

When meeting with international business partners, there are always additional factors to take into consideration. Listen on your cassette/CD as Penny and James discuss what they've learned through years of experience.

AVOIDING BLUNDERS

To help expand your skills, so that you avoid insulting, embarrassing or being discourteous to a foreign visitor or when on business in other countries, make a note here of the tips you heard from Penny and James. Record any other tidbits either you or your colleagues have experienced that will help you to be more culturally aware.

Country	DO	DON'T

FACTORS TO BE CONSIDERED/TRAVEL ARRANGEMENTS

Effective written communication is easy when you take the time to consider the results you want. Knowing something about what will motivate the person you are writing to will increase your chances of getting their attention, cooperation and a positive reply. This applies to faxes, as well as letters. Here's a copy of the cover letter Penny faxed to Mr. Garfield when Sun Club made their first contact with him:

TELEFAX
no. 0294 446 73

To: Paradise Cove Hideaway

Attention: Mr. William Garfield
Re: Inquiry

SUN INTERNATIONAL
London, UK

From: Sun Club International,
Penny McCloud
Pages: 2
Date: October 10, 19..
Time: 12:15

Dear Mr. Garfield,

Mr. McBride, who has been a regular customer of your complex for some time and a trusted personal friend of my family for over 30 years, mentioned that you were looking for potential investors in order to expand your hotel operation.

Our Sun Club division is looking into building a new club resort with conference facilities in the Virgin Islands. It seems we have a mutual interest and we would like to arrange a meeting at your earliest convenience to discuss the possibilities of a joint venture.

Enclosed you will find a general background of our company and our Sun Club division to give you an idea of our marketing strategy and needs. If you are interested in discussing this further, we would appreciate a date when you are available to meet with our Senior Executive VP Jonathan Wadsworth and his Special Tasks Coordinator James Thorne. They would enjoy the opportunity to see your hotel first hand and go over any questions you may have concerning our operation.

We look forward to your earliest reply.

Yours faithfully,

Penny McCloud

Penny McCloud
Executive Assistant

Some tips on opening a letter or fax:

When you don't know the person's name, only that it is a man or a woman, use:
Dear Sir, / Dear Madam,

When you know the name use:
Dear Ms. Smith, (this is for married and unmarried women and used when in doubt)
Dear Mrs. Smith, (for married women)
Dear Miss Smith, (for young unmarried women; "Ms." however, is prefered nowadays)
Dear Mr. Smith, (for men)

When a letter is not to a particular individual, use:
Dear Sirs, (or Gentlemen,)
Ladies and Gentlemen,

When writing to a particular department or title use:
Dear Customer Relations,
Dear Managing Director,

Or when in doubt use:
To whom it may concern:

Closing a letter or fax:

Polite: *Sincerely yours, Sincerely,* or *Cordially,* (US)
Yours sincerely, (UK, when name is mentioned)
Truly yours, or *Yours Truly,*
Yours faithfully, (UK)

Informal: *Best regards, Kindest (Warmest) regards,* or *Regards,*

If you wish to indicate that additional pages are enclosed or that copies have been sent to other people, you can use the following abbreviations at the bottom of the page:

Encl.: (3)   this means three things mentioned in the letter were sent with it
cc: Ms. Baily   this means that Ms. Baily received a copy also

SKILLS
PREPOSITIONS

Prepositions are used differently in almost every language. Here are a few examples of how prepositions are used in English:

Prepositions of Time
at home, **at** 10 o'clock, **at** breakfast, **at** the age of 6
in the morning, **in** the evening, **in** the summertime
on Monday, **on** July 4th, **on** my birthday
by next week, **by** Saturday, **by** then (*means not later than the time given*)
during the week, **during** the winter (*used for a period of time*)
I work **from** 9 **to** 5. Or I work **from** 9 **till** 5. (*both are correct*)

Prepositions of Position
James stays **at** home and lives **in** a house.
The tea is **on** the table and the cat is **under** the chair.
The plane flies **above** the clouds.
Penny goes **over** the hill on horseback.
If Tom sits **next to** you he is **beside** you.
The car is **in front of** the house and the garden is **behind** the house.

Prepositions of Movement
A train goes **through** a tunnel.
We go **from** here **to** there.
I get **on** and **off** a bus, train, or plane but **in** and **out** of a taxi.
You go **into** a pub and come **out of** it.
Penny travels **by** car, **by** train, **by** plane but goes **on** foot to work.
I step **out of** the taxi **onto** the pavement.
Your book fell **off** the shelf **onto** the floor.
You pick it **up off** the floor.

SKILLS   106
Making travel arrangements

For Penny, making travel arrangements is "a breeze" (*easy*, because she does it so often). But sometimes things can go wrong and then James is on his own. As he enters the terminal at Heathrow and glances at the departures listed on the board above him, he notices that his flight to Madrid has been cancelled. With a sinking feeling he patiently waits in line at the check-in counter. The loudspeaker announces the cancellation and the line becomes even longer.

EXERCISE 3-1 AT THE CHECK-IN COUNTER

Listen to your cassette/CD as James checks in.

Just like James, you have an unexpected delay and want to check in. Put the conversation into the correct order.

EXERCISE 3-2 WRITE A DIALOG

○ Fine. Here's your boarding card, Sir. Row 22 seat A.
○ Good morning. Can I help you?
○ Yes, certainly. Here it is.
○ Thank you very much for your help.
○ You should be at gate 12 by 9:20 at the latest. Have a nice flight.
○ Would you put your luggage on the scales, please?
○ There's no need to hurry now. The flight is delayed until 9:40.
○ Where would you like to sit? Smoking or non-smoking?
○ Only half an hour. We apologize for any inconvenience. May I see your ticket please?
○ I only have hand luggage.

SKILLS

○ When should I be at the gate?

○ Non-smoking please. And if possible a window seat.

○ Yes, I'm in a hurry. I want to check in for the flight to Madrid.

○ Oh. I have an important meeting. How long is the delay?

EXERCISE 3-3 SWEET DREAMS

James finds his way to the waiting lounge after stopping at a travel agency, sits down and makes himself comfortable. He relaxes and begins to let his thoughts wander. He is daydreaming ... but you need to help fill in the right prepositions:

1. ___ Sunday morning James is looking ____ his watch. Where is it?

2. He thinks to himself: I'm sure it's __ my nightstand. He's right. 'Oh no', he yells, I'm late! Penny's plane is arriving __ an hour.

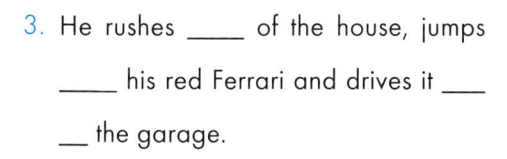

3. He rushes ____ of the house, jumps ____ his red Ferrari and drives it ___ __ the garage.

4. __ _____ __ the house he meets his neighbor Ms. Hall. She asks him __

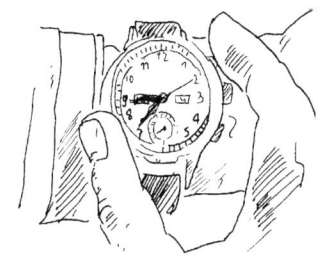

help her because she lost her watch last night when she returned ____ the disco.

5. James replies that he is __ a hurry because he has to be __ the airport __ time.

6. Exactly __ the moment the plane is landing James arrives __ the airport. He leaves his car __ the car park and runs __ the arrival hall.

7. He waits ____ Penny ____ the gate. Penny hurrys _____ the customs control and is delighted when James takes her ____ his arms.

8. Penny tells him that she was thinking a great deal _____ the flight. She says she has made __ her mind to move to the Virgin Islands ...

At this point James is suddenly brought back to reality when the loudspeaker announces the departure of his flight to Madrid. During the flight James casually flips through the inflight magazine and spots a puzzle. See if you can solve it.

SKILLS

EXERCISE 3-4 WHAT TIME IS IT?

A German salesman arrives in the UK on a business trip. At his hotel he phones a taxi company to book a cab for his appointment. He pronounced the time correctly and the taxi company heard him correctly, but the taxi arrived thirty minutes early.

What time did he book the taxi for?
What time did it arrive?

Hint: In Europe it is common to use a 24 hour clock, but it is seldom used in the UK and not at all in the US (the exception is the military forces).

What time is it?   ....

Similar Pairs of words

Here are a few pairs of words so similar that they often cause confusion:

affect	Smoking may **affect** your health.
effect	Smoking can have a dangerous **effect** on your life.
practise (UK)	Pierre will **practise** his presentation before he gives it.
practice	The **practice** will help him build confidence.
advise	Mr. Garfield will **advise** his staff that there may be lay-offs.
advice	He will see his banker for **advice** on how to invest his money.
license	The police are **licensed** to carry handguns.
licence (UK)	You need a fishing **licence** in Scotland to catch salmon.
complement	The colorful scarf **complements** Penny's outfit.
compliment	The men **compliment** Penny on her red hair.

disinterested	**Disinterested** means being unbiased or impartial.
uninterested	**Uninterested** suggests a lack of interest in something.
emigrate	When you move to another country you **emigrate**.
immigrate	When you come from another country you **immigrate.**
principal	She is the **principal** of our college. He is our **principal** supplier.
principle	It's the **principle** of the matter that bothers me the most.
stationery	Penny has her own personal **stationery** for writing letters.
stationary	The satellite is in a **stationary** orbit.
ensure	Sun Club will **ensure** their facilities meet all environmental requirements.
assure	The airline agent **assured** Penny that their staff would not go on strike.
morale	A manager boosts **morale** when he lets his staff have a party.
moral	The **moral** of the story is ...
criticism	Some advertisements have received a lot of **criticism.**
critic	The **critics** think they are in bad taste.

The best way to check words is to use a good dictionary.

GRAFFITI
An expert is like a eunuch in a harem - someone who knows all about it, but can't do anything about it.

SKILLS
Phrasal Verbs

Here are some examples of phrasal verbs with "*to put*":

to put back	When Penny is finished with a book, she **puts** it **back** on the shelf.
	You **put** the clock **back** one hour for daylight-savings time in the winter.
to put forward	The proposal **was put forward** to shorten the work week to 38 hours.
to put in	Sun Club **will put in** a new air-conditioning system.
	Penny **is going to put in** a request for a new computer scanner.
to put in for s. th.	The sales manager **has put in** a request **for** additional staff.
to put off	Many people **are put off** by the stories they hear about the English weather.
	The match **was put off** for a week because of rain.
to put on	James **put on** his jacket to cover the chocolate stain on his shirt.
	James **was** just **putting** Penny **on** about slipping out of the office for a few days. (*"having her on"*, UK)
	Would you please **put** the light **on**?
to put through	Penny **puts** the call **through** to Jonathan's office.
to put up with	Penny **has been putting up with** James' habit of eating chocolate-covered raisins a long time.

Exercise 3-5 Match them up

Now match up the definitions with the correct form of "to put" (remember that some are used more than once):

1. to make a formal request or apply for
2. to return something where it belongs
3. to install
4. to create a bad impression
5. to set the time back
6. to place something on your body
7. to connect a call
8. to submit a request
9. to joke with someone
10. to switch on
11. to postpone something
12. to suggest something
13. to tolerate something

a. to put back
b. to put through
c. to put on
d. to put forward
e. to put in
f. to put off
g. to put in for
h. to put up with

Murphy's Laws
If everything seems to be going well, you obviously don't know what the hell is going on.
In case of doubt, make it sound convincing.

SKILLS
MONEY MATTERS

James has had an eventful trip to Madrid, as you can see from the following fax he sent to Penny from the hotel. First, match the words from list 1 to the correct word from list 2 to make a compound noun. Then use each word pair once to complete James' fax.

EXERCISE 4-1 BUILDING WORD PAIRS

List 1   List 2   **Example: credit card**

1. hand   point   _____
2. VIP   card   _____
3. economy   counter   _____
4. meeting   agent   _____
5. duty-free luggage   _____
6. check-in   lounge   _____
7. travel   class   _____
8. boarding   shop   _____

SKILLS

FAX MESSAGE HOTEL CHA-CHA-CHA

From: James Thorne   Date: January 8, 19..
To: Sun Club, Attn. Penny McCloud
Subject: Madrid trip

MADRID

When I arrived at Heathrow there was a long line at the _____ because my flight had been cancelled. I had to wait half an hour to get a _____ for the next flight to Madrid. The _____ was also full, so I went to the _____ to see what kind of brochures they had for weekend holidays. I was daydreaming too long and there was no time left to go to the _____ and buy the perfume you wanted. Sorry, I'll try in Madrid. Business class was full, so I had to sit in _____. There was no room for my _____ because the woman sitting next to me had brought her cat on board. The seats were so small and uncomfortable, I couldn't work. I think traveling in business class has spoiled me. I had a message sent to José telling him not to wait for me at the _____ and I took a taxi to his office instead.

The hotel you booked is great. See you soon!
Best regards,
James

SKILLS
FINANCES

Money makes the world go round. Businesses have to maintain **financial records** to see if they are making a **profit** so they keep **accounts**. An account is a financial record of information about a group of similar **transactions**, e.g. (exempli gratia, *for example*) sales in one account, costs of raw materials in another and so on. **Accountants** use the information in these accounts to make **financial statements**. These statements are used by management to make decisions such as whether the company can develop a new product or expand. One of the most important statements is the **balance sheet**.

A balance sheet (**asset and liability statement,** US) indicates the *condition of a company* on a specific date and is expressed in *terms of money*. Let's see how an example of a balance sheet for the Virgin Islands Sun Club might look in the future and what each section means:

Hope you finished the balance sheet before this happened!

4 SKILLS 116

Sun Club - Virgin Islands Division
Statement of Financial Condition
as of December 31, 19..

ASSETS
(*Assets* are anything of value owned by a company)

Current Assets
(This is cash, or assets that can be quickly turned into cash, such as merchandise to be sold or payments to be received. It can also include stocks and bonds and is also referred to as *securities*. All of these assets are called *liquid assets*. If a company needs more cash they can *liquidate* some of the stocks and bonds.)

Cash:
  Cash on hand $...........
  United Bank   ....
Notes Receivable $..........
Accounts Receivable   ....
Inventory   ....
Prepaid Insurance   ....
Prepaid Expenses   ....

                            Total Current Assets $.............

Fixed Assets
(These are possessions that will be kept and used for a long time such as land, machinery, etc. and are usually *itemized*. They can also be called *capital* or *permanent assets*. New machinery or equipment is valued at cost and, as it is used, the value decreases (*depreciates*), and this *depreciation* is calculated on a yearly basis.)

Machinery and Equipment $.............
Less: Accumulated Depreciation   -   ....
                                                        $.............

Truck and Automobile $.............
Accumulated Depreciation   -   .... $.............

Furniture and Fixtures $.............
(equipment attached to the building)
Less: Accumulated Depreciation   - $.............
                                                  $.............

Buildings $.............
Less: Accumulated Depreciation   -   ....
                                                $.............

Land (no depreciation) $.............

                Total Fixed Assets $.............
                TOTAL ASSETS $.............

The other side of a balance sheet shows the *liabilities* of a company (money that the company owes to banks, for taxes to the government, money for goods that have not yet been paid for, etc.). Let's take a look at the liabilities Sun Club might have:

Sun Club - Virgin Islands Division
Statement of Financial Condition
as of December 31, 19..

LIABILITIES AND CAPITAL
(Owner's *equity* or *net worth*)

Current Liabilities
(These are *debts* which must be paid on demand for goods or materials, the payroll, interest on borrowed money and taxes. These are *short-term liabilities*.)

Accounts Payable	$.............
Accrued Wages (salaries to be paid)	....
Accrued Sales Tax (VAT-British)	....
Accrued Payroll Taxes	....
Accrued Transportation Taxes	....
Customers Deposits	....
Total Current Liabilities	$...............

Long Term Liabilities
(These are debts that do not have to be paid for a long time; ten, twenty or more years. They could include *long-term interest,* as on bonds for example, or a *mortgage* for purchasing property or equipment. A mortgage is guaranteed by the value of the property mortgaged.)

Notes Payable	$.............
Total Liabilities	$...............

Capital

Capital Stock Authorized and Issued	$.............
Retained Earnings 1/1/19..	$.............
Less: Distribution	- ....
Net Profit for Year Ending December 31, 19..	$.............
Retained Earnings 12/31/19..	$.............
Total Capital	$.............

TOTAL LIABILITIES AND CAPITAL $...............

4

SKILLS 118

When a company subtracts its debts from its assets you have the **net worth** of the company or the **owner's equity**. It is equivalent (*equal*) to the stockholders´ equity in a corporation (US) or shareholders´ equity in a public limited company (Plc, UK) and shows the **value** of the stock. It might not be the same value as the stock on the stock exchange and when it is lower, the company is likely to be taken over by another company.

REVIEW

EXERCISE 4-2 MONEY MAKES THE WORLD GO ROUND

Match the words from a financial statement to the phrase that has a similar meaning:

1. transaction
2. asset
3. inventory
4. liquidate
5. fixed asset
6. itemize
7. net worth
8. liability
9. depreciation
10. securities
11. loan
12. insurance

a. assets minus liabilities
b. sell for cash
c. money a company owes
d. coverage for property, person, etc.
e. the value of something you use goes down
f. sale or purchase by a business
g. merchandise or goods on hand in a company
h. when you borrow money with interest
i. a building or furniture, for example
j. stocks and bonds, for example
k. something of value
l. to list items

SKILLS
THE STOCK MARKET

When a company wants to grow it can *issue shares* (a part of the capital of the company) which the general public can buy (*stocks* in the US). The most common are *ordinary shares* or *equities*. When you buy shares in a company you are a *shareholder* (*stockholder,* US) and own part of the company. You can then make or lose money depending on how the company performs. If it makes a *profit,* the company divides it among the shareholders and you receive a *dividend.* A company, or the government, can borrow money from the public by *issuing bonds* which have a *fixed interest rate.*

Shares or stocks and bonds are *traded,* that means bought and sold, on the different stock exchanges (e.g. Wall Street, London, Frankfurt, Tokyo, etc.) every day. The press gives information about the shares of *listed* companies in the *financial section.* The companies are listed in *sectors* (grouped in a category, such as Food, Metal, Commodity (e.g. coffee), Funds, etc.) with the *high* and *low price, change* of price from the day before, the *yield* (how much you receive in dividends per share) and the *price/earnings ratio* (the relationship between the current market price and the profit earned by a company in the last year and often used to compare companies in the same industry).

Imagine you inherit a large sum of money like Mr. Garfield! How would you *invest* it?

BANKING

Banks offer a number of services for individuals and businesses which most people are familiar with. The name and type of service varies from country to country. *Commercial banks* offer their services to everyone through *branches* in most major cities. *Merchant banks* do not deal with the public in general, but *specialize* in serving the needs of *companies* or *corporations.* They can arrange mergers and acquisitions and advise about corporate finances. *Cen-*

tral Banks function as a **bank to the government**, control the banking system in the respective countries and **issue the currency**.

Think about the services your bank offers you as an individual and the services your company has available. Banks now offer such a variety of accounts, including electronic banking, to suit everyone's individual needs that there isn't enough room here to describe all the possibilites.

> **Murphy's Law**
> In order to get a loan, you first have to prove you don't need it.

EXERCISE 4-3 AT THE BANK

Here are some common banking terms Penny uses in her everyday transactions. Choose a word or word pair from the following list and fill in the text, using each item only once.

outstanding	balance	account	withdraw	transfers
interest	automatic teller	credit card	debited
statement	cash deposit	credit rating	checks (cheques, UK)

1. Penny has a bank card which she uses to _____ money from an _____ _____. 2. Her _____ at the bank is automatically _____ this amount. 3. Sun Club _____ Penny's salary directly to her account. 4. Or Penny can make a ____ _____. 5. Once a month Penny receives a _____ showing the _____ of her account. 6. Penny can write _____ or use her _____ ____ to pay for goods. 7. You need a sound _____ to get a credit card.

SKILLS

8. The credit card company sends Penny a monthly statement showing the _____ balance to be paid. 9. If Penny only makes a partial _____, she will have to pay _____ on the balance.

Penny keeps this as a reminder with her credit cards:
Credit cards have made buying easier but paying harder.

More on Communication

Telex and E-mail (between computers) messages often use a lot of abbreviations to save time. Sometimes they are not easy to understand. You need to look at the whole sentence to understand the meaning. Often the vowels of words are left out and these words are often missing:

- articles (a, an, the)
- prepositions (in, at, on, etc.)
- pronouns (we, you, they, etc.)
- parts of the verb "to be" (is, are, was, were, etc.)

You'll find a complete list of abbreviations in the index that you can refer to whenever necessary.

SKILLS

EXERCISE 4-4 WHAT DOES THE MESSAGE REALLY SAY?

What are the complete messages of the following?

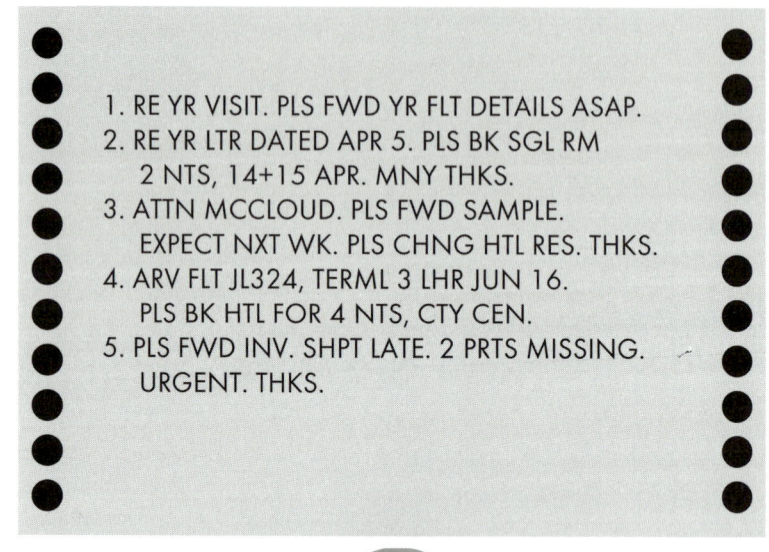

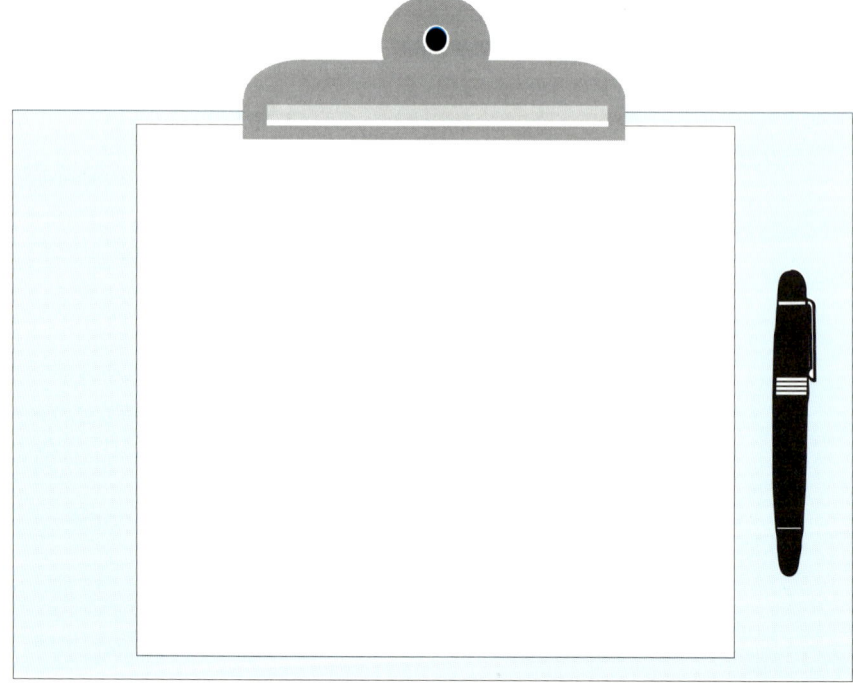

1. RE YR VISIT. PLS FWD YR FLT DETAILS ASAP.
2. RE YR LTR DATED APR 5. PLS BK SGL RM 2 NTS, 14+15 APR. MNY THKS.
3. ATTN MCCLOUD. PLS FWD SAMPLE. EXPECT NXT WK. PLS CHNG HTL RES. THKS.
4. ARV FLT JL324, TERML 3 LHR JUN 16. PLS BK HTL FOR 4 NTS, CTY CEN.
5. PLS FWD INV. SHPT LATE. 2 PRTS MISSING. URGENT. THKS.

SKILLS
Phrasal Verbs

Here is another common phrasal verb, this time **"to take"**

be taken aback	José **was taken aback** when James said he knew about Mr. Garfield's finances.
take after	Penny **takes after** her father. He has red hair too.
take care of	The teller **will take care of** James' transaction at the bank in Madrid.
take down	When James calls Penny, she **takes down** his messages.
take in	It is important not **to be taken in** by stockbrokers.
take off	James *can't* **take off** his jacket because his shirt has a chocolate stain.
	The plane **has** just **taken off**.
	José **is going to take** two weeks **off** this summer for a vacation.
take on	Sun Club **will not take on** new employees in the Virgin Islands Club.
take out	James **is taking** the beautiful bank teller **out** to dinner.
	James **has been taking** chocolate stains **out** of his shirts for years.
take over	José **took over** the Spain branch of Sun Club last year.
take up	After living in China, James **took up** the habit of drinking hot water.
	The teller **took** James **up** on his offer of dinner and shopping.
	Jonathan said he **would take up** the question of overtime at the next meeting.

Exercise 4-5 Match them up

Now match the definition with the correct form of "*to take*" (remember some are used more than once):

1. to be surprised or shocked
2. to depart (planes, trains, etc.)
3. to raise a topic
4. to write down information
5. to be fooled or deceived
6. to remove clothing
7. to resemble or look like someone
8. to stay away from work
9. to give employment
10. to entertain someone
11. to accept an offer
12. to remove a spot
13. to assume control
14. to start something

a. to take off
b. to be taken aback
c. to take up
d. to take care of
e. to take over
f. to take in
g. to take after
h. to take on
i. to take out
j. to take down

HUMAN RESOURCES

Many companies decide to use an **executive search consultant** (or *headhunter*) when they need to **recruit** senior mangagement. Another alternative is a **recruitment agency** or **advertising** the position in a newspaper. **Candidates** who are interested can **apply** for the job by sending a **curriculum vitae** (from Latin, meaning the course of one's life; **CV** for short) or a **résumé** (US), accompanied with a **cover letter**. The company draws up a **short-list** of the candidates they have found suitable, who will then be invited to attend an **interview**.

Your CV should be carefully prepared in order to represent you in the best possible light and tailored to the needs required by the position you are applying for. It should include your *personal details, position sought, employment record, education, references* and any other information that highlights your abilities, such as *professional memberships, awards, publications, additional skills*, etc.

Here's a look at the chocolate finger-printed CV from Otto Huber that James read on the plane. Since requirements vary from country to country, it follows a basic format that displays the information in a clear, concise and readable manner.

Otto Huber
Grand International Hotel
Schnitzelgasse 10, Suite 213
81373 München
Tel. 089-56279 ext. 213

Born: July 4, 1956
Nationality: Swiss
Marital Status: Single

January 8, 19..

CURRICULUM VITAE

Education: 1980: Degree in Hotel Management from the Golden Spoon College of Hotel Management, Zurich, Switzerland.
....
.... (earlier schooling)
....

Professional Experience: 1990 to present: General Manager, Grand International Hotel Responsible for ...

1985-1990: Resident Manager, Ritz Hotel, Rome, Italy Handled all ...
1981-1985: Food and Beverage Manager, Four Season's Hotel, Toronto, Canada. Supervised ...
1969-1981: Management, Reception, Bookkeeping, etc. in parent's ski hotel, Yodel Inn, St. Martin, Switzerland

Additional Skills: Fluent in German, English, Italian and French
Experienced in the conception, organization and execution of PR-functions and conferences
Computer friendly

Interests: Sports: Skiing, Hang-gliding, Climbing, Sailing
Chess, Photography

References:
Harold Townsend	Salvatore Calfiero
General Manager	Director
Four Season's Hotel	Ritz Hotel

Other references furnished upon request

SKILLS

A cover letter (or **letter of application**) can be just as important as your CV because this is your first direct contact with a prospective employer. A well-written letter highlighting aspects of your educational background and business experience that relate directly to the position, will be sure to capture the reader's interest. The purpose is to convince the employer to grant you an interview. You should also include where you heard about the job, explain why you are interested in the position, how your qualifications match the needs of the company and when you would be available for an interview.

Because Otto was approached by a headhunter, he didn't send a typical cover letter along with his CV to the Sun Club Personnel Department. But it would be helpful to see what a typical cover letter looks like, so, here's a copy of one that Penny sent when she originally applied for a position at Sun Club. Fill in the blanks with the correct form of the following verbs:

SKILLS

EXERCISE 5-1 APPLYING FOR A JOB

familiarize/employ/look forward to/supervise/handle/experience/please/
appear/speak/catch/accustom/follow

Penny McCloud
Address
Date of Letter

Sun International
Sun Club Division
Address

Dear Ms. Thompson,

Having _____ a) the expansion of Sun International into the tourist industry, your advertisement for the position of Executive Secretary in the Sun Club Division, which _____ b) in the Guardian on Saturday, immediately _____ c) my attention.

Although I am presently _____ d) in a challenging position with a tour operator, the firm I work for offers very little room for advancement. Because I ____ e) several languages, it has been my intention to seek a positon in an international firm where my talents could be put to better use.

My work experience has _____ f) me with all aspects of office administration, including the_____ g) of staff and the conception of office trainee programs.

_____ h) to working independently, _____ i) in dealing with tourism-oriented products and enthusiastic about working with people, I would be _____ j) to be a part of your expanding team.

I kindly request that this application be _____ k) confidentially and would appreciate the opportunity to answer any further questions you might have about me. I ___ _____ __ l) hearing from you soon.

Yours faithfully,
Penny McCloud

SKILLS

Here are some useful phrases for an interview:

I have been working for ... (*firm's name*) for ... (*number*) years.

.... (*firm's name*) is a/an (*type*) .... firm.

It is based in ... (*where*) and has subsidiaries throughout ....(*where*)

Its annual ...(*output, turnover, profit margin*) is ... and it employs around .... (*type of employees and number*)

It/We export ... (*what*) annually to .... (*where*)

My particular area of responsibility is ... / I am responsible for ...

GRAFFITI
If God really made everything, I'd say he has a quality control problem

SKILLS

RENTING A CAR

There are a bewildering variety of services offered by car rental companies that also vary from country to country depending on the regulations. Here are a few terms to become familiar with:

    unlimited mileage   third-party   groups   categories
    mileage rate   drop-off   pick-up   collision damage waiver
                    fully comprehensive insurance

Fill in the above terms in the following paragraph:

EXERCISE 5-2 AT THE CAR RENTAL

There are two types of car rental. With the first, a customer pays a daily rate plus a _____ _____a) for every mile traveled. The second is more economical for longer journeys and is called _____ _____b). There is no limit to the miles, the customer only pays for gas. Most companies include _____c) insurance, which covers the driver against damage to another vehicle in a collision. _____d) insurance or a _____ _____ _____e) is an additional fee in most countries and insures against damage to the rental car. The cars available to rent come in different _____f) or _____g) depending on their size. A popular service is to _____h) and _____i) the car at the airport.

EXERCISE 5-3 WHAT IS TQM?

During Otto's interview, James and Fritz said they were particularly interested in hearing about how Otto introduced aspects of **Total Quality Management** in the hotel he is presently employed with. Join them now in listening to Otto's description of **TQM** and then answer the following questions to check your comprehension:

1. What was Otto's first step in introducing TQM in his hotel?

2. Why was the word "management" replaced with the word "movement"?

3. Which two elements of TQM did Otto explain in more detail?

4. What did Otto mean when he said, in TQM the customer-supplier relationship goes deeper than just seeing the hotel as the supplier and the guest as the customer?

5. What does TQM require everyone involved in a company to be aware of and to be in agreement on?

6. How does TQM define the word "quality"?

7. What does the "1-10-100 rule" say?

8. Today, what can Otto say six months of TQM has accomplished in his hotel?

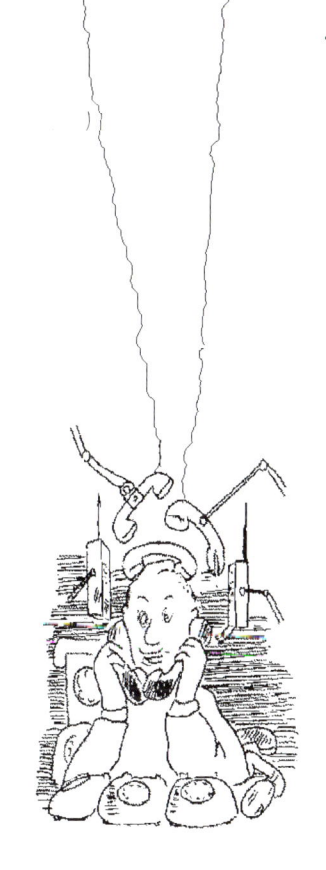

Things to think about:
- What customer-supplier relationship do you see in your business?
- Where could the 1-10-100 rule apply?

Many companies have applied the basics of Total Quality to other aspects such as Total Quality Leadership (TQL), Total Quality Speed (TQS), Total Quality Facilitation (TQF), Total Quality Maturity Path (TQMP), etc.

SKILLS 132

During the interview James and Fritz explained the organizational structure of Sun International to Otto and showed him a chart that looks similiar to this:

ORGANIZATIONAL CHART
SUN INTERNATIONAL

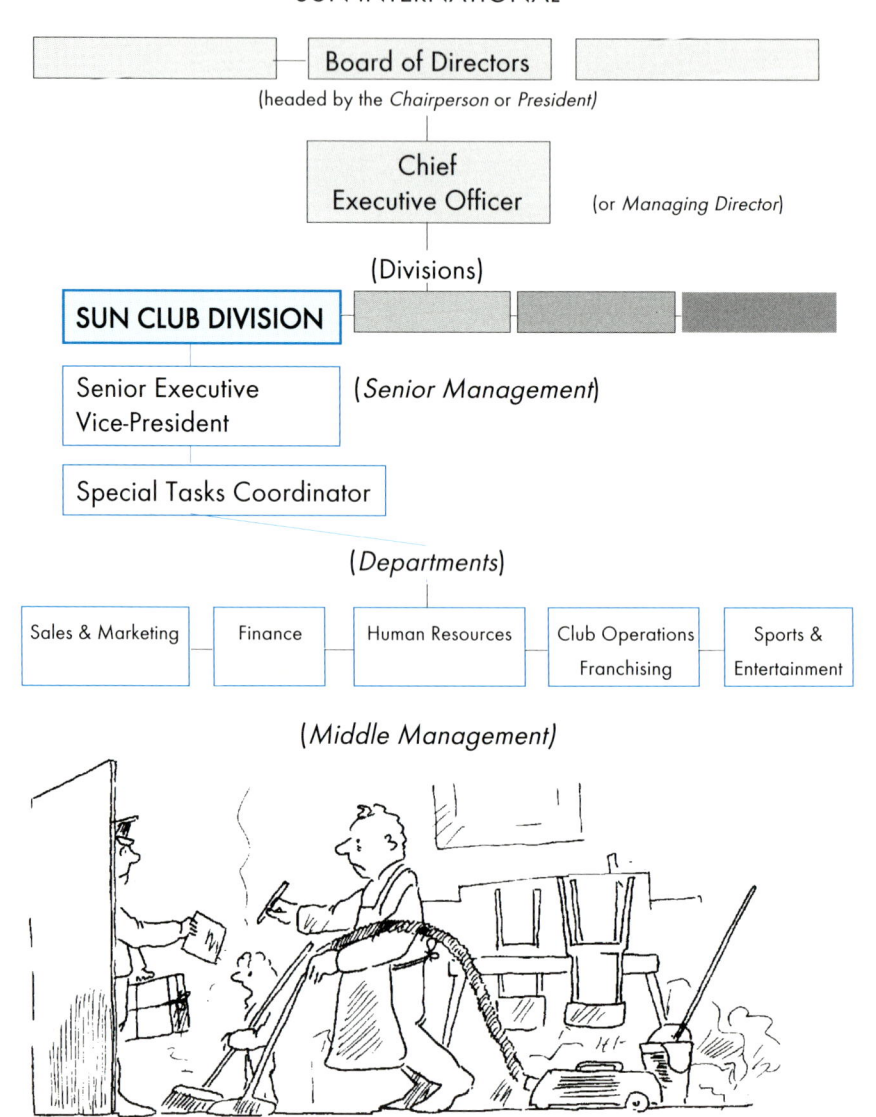

```
┌─────────────┐   ┌──────────────────┐   ┌─────────────┐
│             │───│ Board of Directors│───│             │
└─────────────┘   └──────────────────┘   └─────────────┘
          (headed by the *Chairperson* or *President*)

                    ┌──────────────────┐
                    │      Chief       │
                    │ Executive Officer│   (or *Managing Director*)
                    └──────────────────┘
```

(Divisions)

SUN CLUB DIVISION

| Senior Executive Vice-President | (*Senior Management*) |

| Special Tasks Coordinator |

(*Departments*)

| Sales & Marketing | Finance | Human Resources | Club Operations Franchising | Sports & Entertainment |

(*Middle Management*)

"We're under new mangagement today. Mom's sick."

> **Murphy's Law**
> In any hierarchy,
> each individual rises to his own level of incompetence,
> and then remains there

Phrasal Verbs

Here are some phrasal verbs with *"to call"*:

to call for	The finalizing of the contract **called for** a celebration.
	James **will call for** Penny at eight o'clock.
	People **are calling for** an inquiry into the accident.
to call in	We **have to call in** a plumber to fix the leak in the shower.
	The manufacturer **has called in** model 32 because of defects.
to call off	They **were calling off** the soccer match due to rain.
to call on	James **would call on** Fritz at his office.
	The CEO **has been calling on** all of us to help improve office morale.
to call out	James heard his name **called out** on the loudspeaker.
	Many doctors **are called out** in the middle of the night.
to call up	James **called** Penny **up** to confirm his schedule.

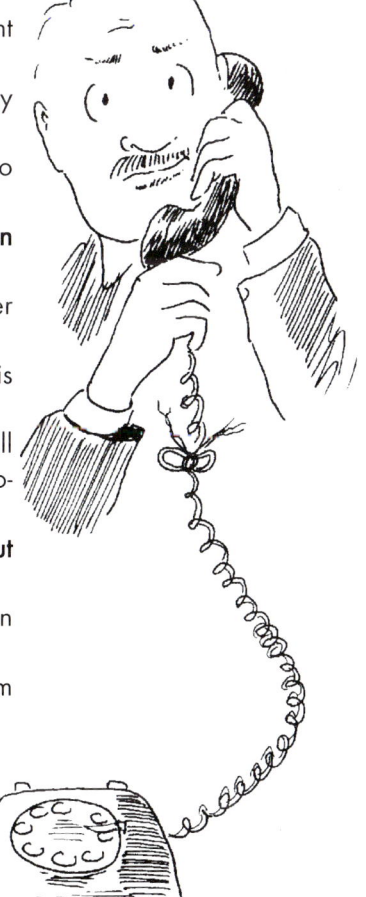

SKILLS

EXERCISE 5-4 MATCH THEM UP

Now match up the definition with the correct form of *"to call"* (Remember some are used more than once.):

1. to telephone
2. to cancel
3. to collect someone
4. to ask or appeal to s.o. for help
5. to require
6. to summon someone or something
7. to visit someone
8. to ask an expert to come
9. to speak in a loud voice
10. to ask for the return of something
11. to demand

a) to call for
b) to call in
c) to call off
d) to call on
e) to call out
f) to call up

BODY LANGUAGE BLUNDERS (*mistakes*)

An American sales executive made a series of presentations to some big clients in Australia. Afterwards, an Australian associate asked how it had gone. The American gave the "thumbs up" sign, meaning "great!". The associate never spoke to him again. Apparently in Australia a thumbs up sign means just the opposite.

In many countries people wave with their palms out, but in Greece this is a serious insult.

On a business trip to Tokyo a foreign executive gave the OK sign when his Japanese host described the restaurant where they would be eating dinner. The host replied, "It's not too expensive." In Japan, making a circle with your fingers means "money". Good thing he wasn't in Brazil or Germany. There the "OK" gesture means something worse than the thumbs up sign in Australia.

SKILLS

In the UK a "V" sign with the palm forward is a V for Victory or "Yes" or "Yeah!". But a V with the palm facing yourself is not something you do in polite company.

In Germanic countries such as Germany, Austria and Switzerland, you do not keep your fingers crossed for luck. You tuck your thumb into your palm when wishing luck.

What sort of interesting things have you learned on your business travels?

live long an prosper (Starship Enterprise)

MARKETING AND ADVERTISING

> The purpose of a business is to get and keep a customer.
> THEODORE LEVITT

Marketing and advertising specialists carry out **research**, or **studies**, to help define their objectives and to find out more about their **target groups**. People who share a common interest, need or desire are a **market**. Many different categories are used on a **market research questionnaire** to divide the market into **groups**. As Adriana mentioned to James, *occupation, income, age, level of education, sex, marital status, social class*, etc. are just a few of the **categories**.

Marketing is a collective term for a number of separate techniques available to focus on the needs of your buyer and effectively communicate information about your product to your chosen target group (or groups). The marketing mix is the main instrument companies use to implement their marketing strategies to ensure their product reaches the intended market.

EXERCISE 6-1 MARKETING OUR PRODUCT

Adriana recently held a workshop for her sales force, where she described the four marketing procedures which Sun Club primarily uses. On your cassette/CD listen now to a summary she gave of these procedures which are listed below. Decide which definition she gives fits with each marketing medium.

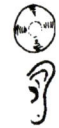

1. Public Relations
2. Advertising
3. Sales Promotion
4. Sales Force

*"Marketing means getting
the right product
at the right time
in the right way
to the right people "*

SKILLS
Describing Trends

In business we often talk about **trends** and use **figures** and **graphs** to describe the changes. When we describe a ***noun,*** such as a product, we use ***adjectives***. When we describe a ***verb*** and *how* something is done, we use an ***adverb***. In English we often add **-ly** to an adjective to create an adverb. For example:

> Production costs rose **sharply** last year.
> Interest has dropped **steadily** over the year.

EXERCISE 6-2 THE TREND IS ...

Decide which of the following commonly-used verbs can be used to describe an increase (up- ↑), a decrease (down- ↓) or a stable situation in business (same- ↔) and place the proper symbol next to it:

a) peak   b) shrink   c) rise   d) fall

e) level off   f) increase   g) decrease   h) improve

i) hold firm   j) recover   k) bottom out   l) slump

m) grow   n) decline   o) remain steady

EXERCISE 6-3 DESCRIBE THE GRAPH

Study the following graph and use an **adjective** form from the following list to complete the description.

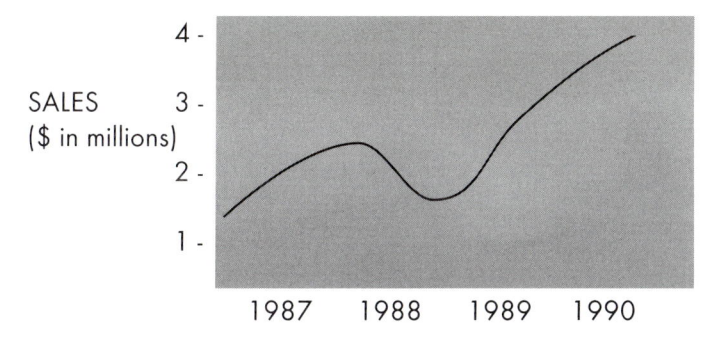

SALES ($ in millions) — graph showing values from 1987 to 1990, rising from about 1.5 to 2.5, dipping to about 1.5 in 1989, then rising to about 4 in 1990.

SKILLS

slightly steadily immediately slowly sharply suddenly
gradually dramatically unpredictably firmly initially adversely
absolutely temporarily considerably

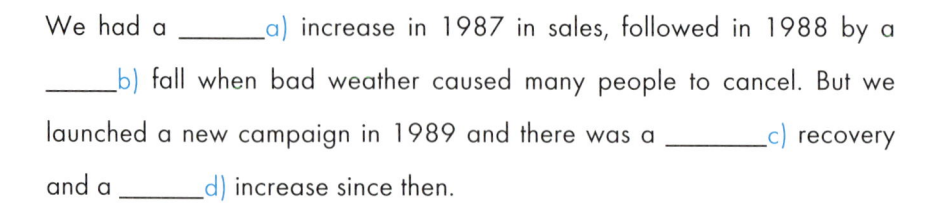

We had a _____a) increase in 1987 in sales, followed in 1988 by a _____b) fall when bad weather caused many people to cancel. But we launched a new campaign in 1989 and there was a _____c) recovery and a _____d) increase since then.

EXERCISE 6-4 DESCRIBE HOW IT CHANGED

Now study the following graph and use the **adverb** form of the above adjectives to complete the description.

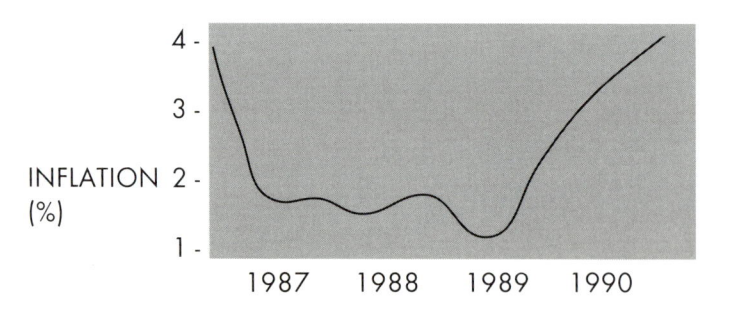

Inflation fell _____a) in 1987 and then continued to decrease _____b) for the next two years. In 1989 it went down _____c) but rose _____ d) in 1990 because of interest rates.

If you need to explain why a change took place, you can use expressions such as:

The decline in .... *resulted in* a decrease in our market share.
  led to
  shows
The growth in ... *resulted from* the increase in our market share.
  was due to

SKILLS
Spelling

This is often confusing in English because many words are pronounced similarly but are spelled differently. It's a good idea to keep a list of words you have difficulty with. Test yourself frequently by trying to use them in a sentence that applies to an everyday activity. Refer to a good dictionary when you are unsure.

EXERCISE 6-5 FINISH SPELLING THE WORDS

Is it an "a" or an "e" that is missing in the following words?

a) confid_nt   b) insolv_nt   c) signific_nt   d) curr_nt
e) consist_nt f) domin_nt   g) conveni_nt   h) perman_nt
i) reluct_nt   j) extravag_nt k) redund_nt   l) const_nt
m) compet_nce n) advancem_nt o) tal_nt

Word Stress

Some verbs and nouns are the same in English, such as *to dream a dream*. Some sound alike, such as *to affect an effect* and others are spelled the same, but stressed differently, such as *to obJECT to an OBject*. Here is a short list of some that may still confuse you:

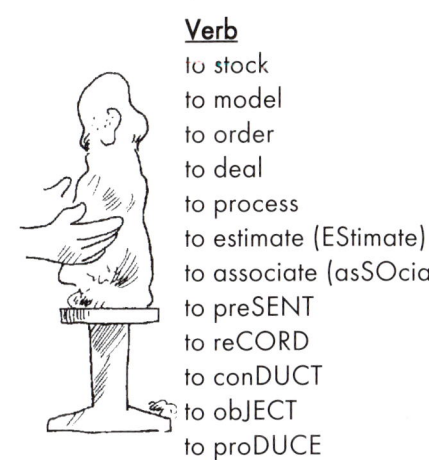

Verb	Noun
to stock	the stock
to model	a model
to order	an order
to deal	a deal
to process	a process
to estimate (EStimate)	an estimate (EStimit)
to associate (asSOciate)	an associate (asSOci it)
to preSENT	a PREsent
to reCORD	a REcord
to conDUCT	the CONduct
to obJECT	an OBject
to proDUCE	a PROduct
to PHOtograph	a phoTOGrapher

Murphy's Law
If you try to please everyone, nobody will like it.

SKILLS

EXERCISE 6-6 LISTENING TO THE PRONOUNCIATION

Listen carefully now on your cassette/CD to how each word is pronounced in the following sentences and then read them aloud to yourself to check your pronunciation.

1. Sun Club **stocks** plenty of golf balls at their clubs. Tennis balls are out of **stock** at the moment.
2. The resort is **modeled** after the original "Hideaway Cove". Mr. Garfield has a **model** of it.
3. James **orders** lunch in Rome. The waiter takes the **order**. Mr. Garfield **ordered** new air-conditioning. His **order** will take 2 months to deliver and install.
4. James has learned how **to deal** with difficult customers by offering them a good **deal**.
5. Penny will **process** the paperwork quickly. The **process** normally takes one day.
6. Mr. Garfield gave Sun Club **an estimate** of the costs for renovation. He **estimated** that they would need a minimum of 6 months to finish.
7. Sun Club is **associated** with fun in the sun. James' **associates** admire his talents.
8. Pierre will **present** the new Sun Club in the Virgin Islands to his clients. James bought Penny a **present** in Spain.
9. The Rolling Stones **recorded** a new **record** this year. It sold a **record** number in Japan.
10. Adriana **conducted** a survey of Sun Club's target groups. She cannot control her dog's **conduct** when visitors arrive at her house.
11. Adriana **objected** to using television to advertise Sun Club. Her husband collects **objects** of art from Africa.
12. Sun Club's project **produces** less pollution because they use earth-friendly **products.** They always try to use fresh **produce** in their clubs.
13. James has a **photograph** of Penny in his wallet that was taken by a **photographer** in Scotland.

JOKE

"My wife says she will leave me if I don't throw out my computer."
"Oh, I'm sorry to hear that."
"So am I. I'll miss her."

SKILLS

Endorsements

Many companies often use *celebrities* to endorse their products. Although it's very popular in Japan to use well-known actors, actresses and sports figures from the US, at home in the US they rarely do commercials because it is a sign that their career is on the way down and they need money. A company might expect a personality to:
- make appearances to promote a product at trade fairs, in-store or other events.
- wear a company logo on an article of clothing.
- appear in a commercial or in a mail-order catalogue.
- to personalize the company´s products with their signature.

Who do you think James had in mind to promote Sun Club?

Phrasal Verbs

Here are a few phrasal verbs with "*to go*":

to go ahead	Adriana **will go ahead** with the advertising campaign.
to go along with	Mr. Gionelli **is going along with** their ideas for the ad.
to go back on	James **went back on** his promise to stop eating chocolate.
to go by	Don't **go by** my watch. It's off (*out, UK*) by 10 minutes.
	James watched the traffic **go by** before he risked crossing the street. (It's Rome, remember!)
to go down	The sun **went down** at 7:40 p.m.
	The medicine **goes down** better with sugar.
	Her weight **has gone down** 5 kilos since she began her diet.
to go for	Small dogs usually **go for** the postman's leg.
to go in for	James **has been going in for** chocolate-covered raisins lately.
to go into	Adriana didn't **go into** all the details about the new ad agency.
to go off	The alarm **went off** late and Penny overslept.
	She **has gone off** drinking red wine since her holiday in Spain.
to go on	Please **go on**, I'm very interested.
	The manager doesn't have enough information **to go on**.
	What's **going on** here?
to go through	I hope I never have **to go through** that examination again!
	She **had gone through** all her papers looking for the report.
	After a series of negotiations, the deal **went through**.
to go up	Inflation **has been going up** 2% every year.
	James **went up** to the car rental counter and inquired about a car.
	The building **went up** in flames.
to go with	Pickles **would go** well **with** peanut butter on a sandwich.

Exercise 6-7 Match them up

Now match up the definition with the correct form of *"to go"* (remember to use some of them more than once):

1. to attack
2. to agree with a suggestion
3. to continue
4. to examine or review
5. to use as a guide
6. to be well-received
7. to combine well with
8. to talk about in detail
9. to go past
10. to happen
11. to approach
12. to proceed or continue with s.th.
13. to begin to dislike
14. to rise or increase
15. to set (the sun)
16. to decrease
17. to experience
18. to be especially interested in
19. to suddenly make a noise
20. to start to burn
21. to be guided by
22. to be completed successfully
23. to not keep a promise

a) to go ahead
b) to go along with
c) to go back on
d) to go by
e) to go down
f) to go for
g) to go in for
h) to go into
i) to go off
j) to go on
k) to go through
l) to go up
m) to go with

SKILLS
PR AND PRESENTATIONS

Many things have to be considered and carefully planned when you give a presentation of your company, introduce a new product or introduce a new system. If you have a lot of complicated information to explain, visual aids can make your presentation easier to understand and more interesting. Use the most appropriate aids available and those that you feel most confident with. Look at the following list and match these items commonly used in a presentation with the pictures shown below:

EXERCISE 7-1 PREPARING FOR A PRESENTATION

slide projector   screen   table (with figures)   graph
overhead projector (OHP)   pie chart   notes   handout
marker/felt pen   pointer   remote control   transparencies
sales folder   bar chart   flipchart   microphone   podium   video

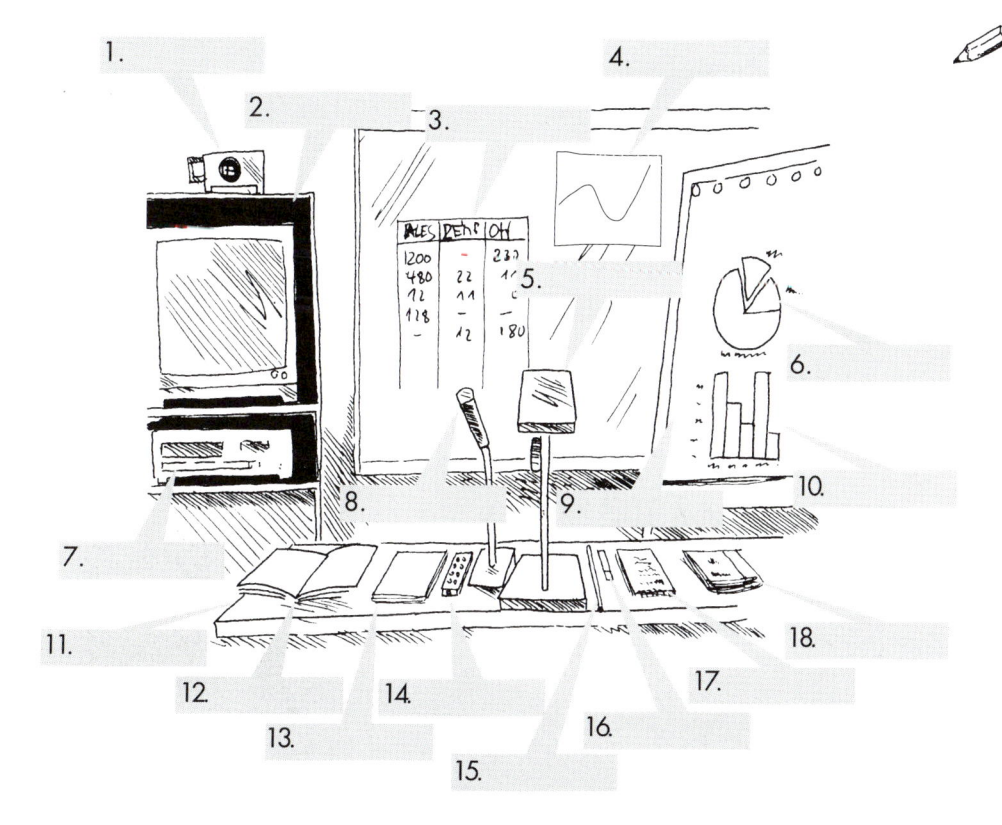

SKILLS

Pierre handed Penny the cue cards which he had prepared for his presentation. He used a number of useful phrases that provided a structure for his presentation and made it easier for the audience to follow him. They can signal to your audience that you have reached the end of a point, that you are moving on to the next point, that you are giving an example, and so on. In the following examples, you will find many expressions appropriate for your next presentation.

INTRODUCING A TOPIC

I'd like to begin by telling (showing, demonstrating, etc.) ...
First of all, ...
Let me start with ...
As you know ...

REACHING THE END OF A POINT

We've looked at ...
As you can see ...
As I have explained ...

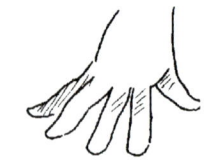

MOVING ON TO THE NEXT POINT

Now I'd like to show you ...
Let's move on to ...
Next, let's turn to ...
As this diagram (graph, transparency, etc.) *shows ...*

DEVELOPING OR ANALYSING A POINT

I'd like to suggest some distinct advantages of ...
Let's look at this in more detail ...
What does that mean for us?
I should point out that ...
I'd like to remind you that ...
As I will explain ...

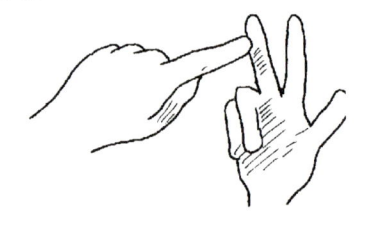

GIVING AN EXAMPLE

I'd like to demonstrate ...
For example, ...
To illustrate this point ...
A good example is ...

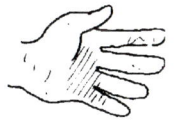

DEALING WITH QUESTIONS NOW OR LATER

I'd like to invite you to ask questions now ...
I'll come back to this question later, but now ...
We'll examine this question later in more detail ...
I'd like to emphasize that ...

SUMMARIZING / CONCLUDING

I'd like to close by saying ...
Let's recap ...
As I have explained ...
I'd like to add that ...

Pierre explained the objectives of his presentation to Penny and told her a little bit about the audience. Whenever you give a presentation, you have to know whom you'll be addressing and what you want to achieve. Ask yourself whether you want to inform, persuade, train or entertain your audience? After Pierre recapped the main points of how to give a presentation, James finished up by giving Penny some additional tips on delivery. In addition to speaking slowly and making pauses, he also told her to:

- speak clearly
- use simple words and short sentences
- avoid slang and abstract concepts
- give a signal when changing the direction of your presentation

Try to avoid complicated words.

SKILLS

EXERCISE 7-2 GIVING PRESENTATIONS

Now listen on your cassette/CD to a summary of the six steps James told Penny she needed to become a strong and confident public speaker. Afterwards, answer the following questions:

1. How can you make tension work for you?
   How can you release tension before going on stage?

2. Give a few examples of a good opening.

3. How can you develop good eye contact with your audience?

4. What are some important things to remember when using visual aids?

5. In dealing with a question, what should you do first?
   How can you encourage "friendly" questions and discourage "unfriendly" ones? What can you say if you need time to think?
   What will gain you credibility if you can't answer the question?

6. What should you do over and over again before giving a presentation?
   What attitude should you adopt, just in case something goes wrong?

Phrasal Verbs

Here are some phrasal verbs with *"to make"*:

to make into	They **will make** the hotel room **into** a temporary office.
to make out	Pierre's handwriting was so bad that Penny **couldn't make** it **out**. Please **have** the check **made out** to me personally.
to make up	James **made up** his mind to stop eating chocolate. They would kiss and **make up** after a quarrel. Pierre **has been making up** excuses why he couldn't see Brigit.
to make up for	Penny **was making up for** lost time by practising the presentation.

SKILLS

EXERCISE 7-3 MATCH THEM UP

Now match up the definitions with the correct form of "*to make*":

1. to manage to see, hear, etc. clearly
2. to invent a story
3. to compensate for something
4. to write a check
5. to become friends again after an argument
6. to decide
7. to transform

a. to make into
b. to make out
c. to make up
d. to make up for
e. to make up one´s mind

> The reason why we have two ears and only one mouth is that we may listen more and talk less
>
> ZENO

INTRODUCING A GUEST SPEAKER

At times, your job may require you to introduce a guest speaker or to congratulate someone in English. When speaking in a foreign language, the hardest part is knowing how best to begin. Here are a few useful openers that might help you, taken from the International Public Speaking course by Peter R. Heigl:

It is my great pleasure to introduce / to welcome today ...

For the ... years he / she has been working
    in the field of ...
    for the company / institution ...
    He / She is currently / presently ...
    He / She has published articles / books on ...
    His / Her special interest lies in ...

Please welcome ...
Please join me in welcoming ...

CONGRATULATORY SPEECH

It is with great pleasure that we are gathered here today ...
to congratulate our dear colleague / guest
on the occasion of his / her ...
- promotion
- engagement
- birthday

... has been working / has worked with us since ... (date)
for ... (number) years.

We have always treasured him / her for his / her ...
- commitment
- expertise in ...
- great sense of humor
- hard work

We wish him / her well ...
all the best ...
- for the future
- in retirement
- in his / her new job

Let us drink to the health of our colleague (raise your glass)
Dear ... , to your health!

The Pareto Secret

This is named after Wilfredo Pareto, an economist at the turn of the century. He observed that 20% of the population in Italy controlled 80% of the wealth. This was then applied to other areas:

- 20% of your clients account for 80% of your sales
- 20% of your clients make 80% of the complaints
- 20% of the workers do 80% of the work
- 20% of a newspaper contains 80% of the information
- 80% of the dirt found at home is in 20% of the area

TIME	RESULTS
20%	80%

This is a general percentage of 80:20. Think about how this affects your professional and private life and what impact it could have on your effectivity.

We learn from our mistakes. But sometimes we don't always realize we've made one. Here are some words that are frequently misused in English. Choose the correct one in each of the following sentences. You can develop a feeling for what "sounds" right by using each word in a sentence of your own.

EXERCISE 7-4 PICK THE RIGHT ONE

1. I am **interested / interesting** in your new advertising campaign.
2. James is **sensitive / sensible** to criticism from Penny about his chocolate habit.
3. The cost of **life / living** is going down in some countries.
4. She studied **economy / economics** at the university.
5. My bank agreed to **borrow / lend** me the money for a new house.
6. We expect the inflation rate to **raise / rise** by 2% this year.
7. I'll give you my **receipt / recipe** for pumpkin pie.
8. Can you **say / tell** me the difference between these two products?
9. James' plane was **postponed / delayed** only 30 minutes.
10. You must **remind / remember** me of the meeting.
11. I'll ask the bank manager for some **advise / advice** about investing.
12. Does the air-conditioning system **confirm / conform** to the new regulations?
13. You are not allowed to read **confidential / confident** letters.
14. Penny is a very **conscious / conscientious** employee.
15. Please send me your **price / prize** list.
16. Can you explain **me / to me** why the meeting was cancelled?
17. James has been with the company **for / since** 14 years.
18. The cost of living is higher in Japan **than / as** England.

> Results come from doing the RIGHT thing,
> not from doing things right.
>
> PETER DRUCKER
>
> This means that someone who is *efficient* **does things right.**
> And someone who is *effective* **does the right thing.**

SKILLS

Adjectives and their opposites can be used to describe your products or services. An adjective can have more than one opposite depending on the context. For example, the opposite of *short* could be **long** or **tall**. Sometimes the opposites are formed by adding the prefix **dis-**, **un-**, **in-**, **im-**, or **ir-**. Complete the sentences below using the opposites of the words in brackets:

EXERCISE 7-5 USING THE OPPOSITES

permanent	uneconomical	impossible	made	inefficient
(temporary)	(economical)	(possible)	(lost)	(efficient)
agreed	boring	unreliable	failed	irresponsible
(disagree)	(interesting)	(reliable)	(succeeded)	(responsible)

1. The new secretary is _____ because she can't type or take shorthand.
2. Listening to a long speech can be _____.
3. The new advertising campaign is _____.
4. When he doesn't fulfill his duties he is _____.
5. Our new sales concept has _____.
6. The CEO _____ with our new proposal.
7. These sales figures are _____ to meet.
8. He _____ a fortune on the stock market.
9. The job is _____.
10. Drinking and driving is _____.

HANDLING COMPLAINTS/COMMUNICATION

A golden rule of communication:

> What may seem obvious, clear and straightforward to you,
> is not necessarily so to your listener.

Answering machines

How often have you made a call, only to be greeted by a recorded message? Many people have a phobia about talking to a machine. When making **any** phone call, know what you want to say beforehand so that you will be prepared for anything. Listen on your cassette/CD to the recorded messages left on Sun International's answering machine. On the pad below, make a note of the important information of each phone call:

EXERCISE 8-1 WHO'S CALLING?

Name of caller	Tel. no.	Details
1.	....	....
		....
		....
		....
2.	....	....
		....
		....
		....
3.	....	....
		....
		....
		....

SKILLS 152

Telephoning
Herausforderung

Speaking on the telephone can be a challenge even in your own language because you can only **hear** the person you're dealing with. It's important to speak clearly, concisely, to avoid long silences and to use a warm and enthusiastic voice. Smile when you speak. The person you're talking to can feel it.

Here are some standard expressions in English that can be used for telephoning. In the following examples taken from the text, find the lead-in phrase from the list on the left. More than one phrase on the left can be correct. You may find many of them useful for **your** next telephone conversation.

EXERCISE 8-2 ONE MOMENT PLEASE

INTRODUCING

✗ This is ... I'd like to speak to ...
My name is ...
✗ Who's calling please? ✗
Max Hoofddorp. How can I help you?
Speaking. (when you are the person asked for, it means "That's me".)
Could I have your name please.

1. James:
James Thorne _speaking_.

HOLDING

✗ Just a moment. I'll put you through.
Hold the line, please.
✗ The line's busy. Will you hold?
One moment please.

2. Gulliver's Travel:
Our agents are busy. _Hold_ _the line pls_ or try again ...

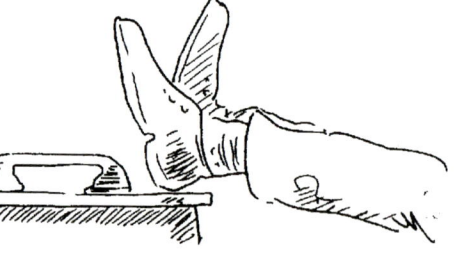

SKILLS

NEGATIVE RESPONSE

I'm afraid he's on holiday.
I'm afraid he's rather tied up.
I'm sorry, she's in a meeting.
I'm afraid he's not in the office at the moment.
She's no longer with us. Can someone else help you?

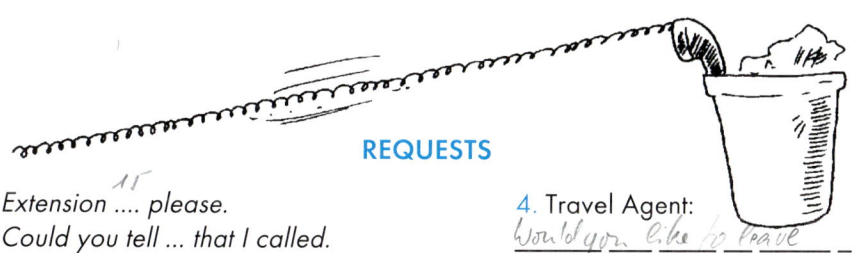

3. Travel Agent:
Oh, _I am afraid he is rather tied up_ at the moment.

REQUESTS

Extension _15_ .... please.
Could you tell ... that I called.
Would you like to leave a message?
Could you take a message, please?
Could you ask ... to call me back, please?
I'm sorry, could you repeat that, please?

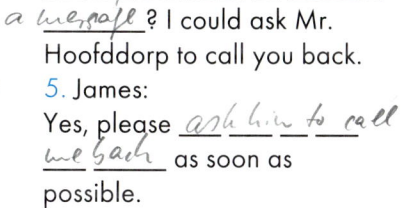

4. Travel Agent:
Would you like to leave a message? I could ask Mr. Hoofddorp to call you back.

5. James:
Yes, please _ask him to call me back_ as soon as possible.

GAINING TIME

Really? (asks for more details)
Sorry? (asks to repeat what was said)
Could you say that slowly, please.
Can you give me more details ...
I'm afraid the connection is bad.
Could you repeat that please.

6. James:
You can gain time by using expressions like, "_really_" or "Can you give me more details ..."

7. A question like: "_Could you say that slowly_, so I can make a note of it please?"

Note:
Sometimes expressions in British and American English have completely different meanings. For example, a British operator will ask "*Are you through?*" to see if you are connected and you can then **begin** your call. An American operator who asks "*Are you through?*" wants to know if the call is **finished.**

SKILLS 154
COMPLAINTS

Handling a complaint is easy if you know how to proceed. James gave Jannie some useful tips. See if you can place them in the order they should be used when responding to a complaint on the telephone:

EXERCISE 8-3 ANSWERING A TELEPHONE COMPLAINT

5 a. Express thanks for the complaint. (Explaining that this is the only way mistakes can be avoided in the future, stresses the positive aspect of a complaint.)

3 b. Write down the details and repeat them.

6 c. Mention earlier positive experiences of the clients (if they exist), and point out common interests. (This puts the complaint in the background and good business relations in the foreground.)

2 d. Convey sympathy, understanding and regret.

1 e. Let the client talk and get everything off his chest.

4 f. Promise a rapid response. ("I'll take care of it personally" always sounds good.)

Murphy's Law
There's never time to do it right,
but there's always time to do it over again

SKILLS

EXERCISE 8-4 TELEPHONE CROSSWORD

Complete the typical telephone expressions below to find the key word in number 14 down.

```
          14.
 1.        B A C K
 2.          S O R R Y
 3.            M E S S A G E
 4.          M O M E N T
 5.            B U S Y
 6.   S P E A K I N G
 7.          H O L I D A Y
 8.            C A N
 9.          C A L L I N G
10.            T I E D U P
11.   D E T A I L S
12.            H O L D
13.   E X T E N S I O N
```

1. I'll call him _back_ later.
2. I'm _sorry_. He's out of town.
3. Could I leave a _message_, please?
4. One _moment_ please.
5. I'm afraid his line is _busy_
6. James Thorne, _speaking_.
7. He's on _holiday_ at the moment.
8. _Can_ I help you?
9. Who's _calling_, please?
10. He's _tied up_ at the moment.
11. Could you give me more _details_, please?
12. _Hold_ the line please.
13. What's his _extension_ number, please?

DOWN

14. A key to successful management.

APOLOGIES

In his conversation with James, Mr. Hoofddorp used some standard English responses to apologize. Spoken and written apologies differ slightly. When a letter of complaint is received, a company will send a letter of apology.

The beginning could start with one of the following phrases:
Please accept our sincere apologies for ...
We are very sorry about the delay / mistake / misunderstanding ...
Please accept our apologies for the inconvenience caused by ...
We would like to apologize for ...

You can end the letter with one of the following phrases:
We are anxious to settle this matter to everyone's satisfaction ...
We will naturally send ... free of charge.
We hope that this arrangement will meet with your approval.
We will take the necessary steps to ensure that such a mistake does not occur again.

This is the letter of apology Mr. Hoofddorp wrote in response to the complaint sent by the group who stayed at the Virgin Islands Sun Club:

GULLIVER'S TRAVELS
Address
Telephone/Fax
Date

Company
Address

Re: Complaint ...

Dear Mr. Komduur,

Please accept our sincerest apologies for the false impression one of our agents gave you of the entertainment program offered at the Sun Club facilities in the Virgin Islands. Sun Club was in no way responsible for the misunderstanding.

We realize this matter caused considerable disappointment for your group. We have therefore enclosed tickets for the Amsterdam performance of the magician your group expected to see at Sun Club. Transportation will also be arranged, free of charge.

We hope that this arrangement will meet with your approval.
Anxious to settle the matter to everyone's complete satisfaction, we have taken steps to ensure that such a mistake does not occur again. We have the highest regards for the services Sun Club provides and hope that you will consider using them again in the future.

Yours sincerely,

Max Hoofddorp
President

cc: Sun Club

Phrasal Verbs

Here are some examples of the phrasal verb *"to keep"*:

to keep away	Nothing seems to **keep away** the mosquitoes at night.
to keep back	Is James **keeping** something **back** from Penny?
to keep down	Sun Club **kept** travel expenses **down** last year.
	The Club disco should **keep** the music **down** late at night.
to keep off	The sign at the entrance of the club said: '**Keep off** the grass!'.
to keep on	Penny's cousin hasn't found a job yet, but she'll **keep on** trying.
	Sun Club is going to **keep on** all of Mr Garfield's employees.
	In the US ladies should **keep on** their bikini tops when swimming.
to keep out	No trespassing. **Keep out**!
to keep up	After the disaster Mr. Garfield couldn't afford to **keep up** the payments.
to keep up with	He ran so fast that it was difficult **keeping up with** him.
	James reads the paper every day to **keep up with** the latest news.

EXERCISE 8-5 MATCH THEM UP

Now match up the definition with the correct form of "to keep" (remember to use some more than once):

1. to continue
2. to not tell or reveal information
3. to maintain (payments etc.)
4. to not allow to come near
5. to control
6. to go at the same speed
7. to keep at a low level
8. to continue to employ
9. to not walk on
10. to not allow entrance to s. th.
11. to stay up-to-date
12. to not take off

a) to keep away
b) to keep back
c) to keep down
d) to keep off
e) to keep on
f) to keep out
g) to keep up
h) to keep up with

SKILLS

Here's the best of Murphy's "Table of Handy Office Excuses"

> Excuse me but ...
> 1. ... that's the way we've always done it.
> 2. ... I didn't know you were in a hurry for it.
> 3. ... that's not my department.
> 4. ... that's not my job.
> 5. ... we don't make many mistakes.
> 6. ... I didn't think it was very important.
> 7. ... I wasn't hired to do that.
>
> *Or, when in doubt, mumble. When in trouble, delegate.*

EXERCISE 8-6 PUZZLE

Solve this puzzle by replacing the **first** letter of the **left hand** word and the **last** letter of the **right hand** word with a letter that forms two new words. The word formed in the brackets will complete this:

Example: bed (r) bat

red	bed	r	bat	bar

	let		bat	- - -
- - -	pope		cat	- - -
- - -	sat		top	- - -
- - -	cloud		gale	- - -
- - -	boast		fad	- - -

You are _____ !

This is one of Penny's favorites in her collection of sayings:

- Take the time to work, for it is the price of success.

- Take the time to think, it is the source of strength.

- Take the time to play, it is the secret of youth.

- Take the time to read, it is the seed of wisdom.

- Take the time to be friendly, for it brings happiness.

- Take the time to dream, for it will carry you to the stars.

- Take the time to love, it is the joy of life.

- Take the time to be content, it is the music of the soul.

(Original Irish Text)

ANSWER KEY
SKILLS

Exercise 1-1
a. Dutch b. German c. French d. Italian e. Spanish
f. Scottish g. English h. American
1. Danish, Danes 2. Swedish, Swedes 3. Finnish, Finns
4. Turkish, Turks 5. Polish, Poles

Exercise 1-3
1. head office 2. minutes 3. circulated 4. record 5. corporate
6. resort 7. facilities 8. consider 9. overall 10. resolved
11. critieria 12. strengths 13. innovative 14. competing
15. target 16. basic 17. adjourned 18. scheduled 19. sales

Exercise 1-5
1. i 2. b 3. g 4. l 5. a 6. j
7. k 8. c 9. d 10. h 11. e 12. f

Exercise 2-1
1. b 2. d 3. f 4. a 5. c 6. e

Exercise 2-2
1. Our objective today 2. I fully agree 3. That's correct.
4. I think you're right. 5. maybe you're right. 6. I'm afraid I don't agree
7. That's out of the question! 8. I'm not so sure. 9. I suggest
10. Nevertheless, we could 11. So, what you're saying is
12. In my opinion 13. We have no doubt
14. You have a point 15. let's move on to

Exercise 2-3
1. d 2. b 3. h 4. c 5. f 6. a 7. g 8. e

Exercise 2-4
1. expansion 2. investor 3. digestion 4. blueprints 5. joint venture
6. raw materials 7. authorities 8. renovation 9. negotiation
10. depreciates 11. inventory list 12. red tape 13. upgrade
14. a letter of intent 15. trademark 16. assets

ANSWER KEY

Exercise 3-2

Good morning. Can I help you?
Yes, I'm in a hurry. I want to check in for the flight to Madrid.
There's no need to hurry now. The flight is delayed until 9:40.
Oh. I have an important meeting. How long is the delay?
Only half an hour. We apologize for any inconvenience. May I see your ticket?
Yes, certainly. Here it is.
Would you put your luggage on the scales, please?
I only have hand luggage.
Where would you like to sit? Smoking or non-smoking?
Non-smoking please. And if possible a window seat.
Fine. Here's your boarding card, sir. Row 22 seat A.
When should I be at the gate?
You should be at gate 12 by 9:20 at the latest. Have a nice flight.
Thank you very much for your help.

Exercise 3-3:

1. on, for 2. on, in 3. out, into, out of
4. In front of, to, from 5. in, at, on
6. at, at, in, to 7. for, at, through, into
8. during, up

Exercise 3-4

The salesman booked the taxi for 22.10. It arrived at 21.40 (or twenty to ten). The times sound the same: twenty-two ten, twenty to ten.

Exercise 3-5

1.g 2.a 3.e 4.f 5.a 6.c 7.b 8.e 9.c 10.c 11.f 12.d 13.h

Exercise 4-1

1. hand luggage 2. VIP lounge 3. economy class 4. meeting point
5. duty-free shop 6. check-in counter 7. travel agent 8. boarding card
Fax: 6, 8, 2, 7, 5, 3, 1, 4

Exercise 4-2

1.f 2.k 3.g 4.b 5.i 6.l 7.a 8.c 9.e 10.j 11.h 12.d

ANSWER KEY

Exercise 4-3
1. withdraw, automatic teller 2. account, debited 3. transfers 4. cash deposit 5. statement, balance 6. checks, credit card 7. credit rating 8. outstanding 9. payment, interest

Exercise 4-4
1. In reference to your visit, please forward your flight details to us as soon as possible.
2. In reference to your letter dated April 5th, please book me a single room for 2 nights on the 14th and 15th. Many thanks.
3. Attention McCloud, please forward a sample. I expect it next week. Please change my hotel reservation. Thanks.
4. I am arriving on Flight JL324 at Terminal 3 in London Heathrow airport on June 16th. Please book a hotel accomodation for four nights in the city center.
5. Please forward the invoice. The shipment was late and two parts are missing. It's very urgent. Thank you.

Exercise 4-5
1.b 2.a 3.c 4.j 5.f 6.a 7.g 8.a 9.h 10.i 11.c 12.i 13.e 14c

Exercise 5-1
a) followed b) appeared c) caught d) employed e) speak f) familiarised g) supervising h) accustomed i) experienced j) pleased k) handled l) look forward to

Exercise 5-2
a) mileage rate b) unlimited mileage c) third-party d) fully comprehensive insurance e) collision damage waiver f) groups g) categories h) pick-up i) drop-off

Exercise 5-3
1. To get an external consultant to set up a workshop. 2. To show that TQM is not something imposed on a company from the top, but a movement through the entire company. 3. The "customer-supplier relationship" and the "1-10-100 rule". 4. There are an endless number of working relationships within the staff itself. 5. To be in agreement about the product and its standard of quality. 6. Quality means "suitability for the purpose intended". 7. The 1-10-100 rule says that the earlier a mistake is detected the cheaper

it is to correct. 8. That they are more conscious of what actually takes place in their business.

Exercise 5-4
1.f 2.c 3.a 4.d. 5.a 6.e 7.d 8.b 9.e 10.b 11.a

Exercise 6-1
1.c 2.a 3.d 4.b

Exercise 6-2
a)same b)down c)up d)down e)same f)up g)down h)up i)same j)up k)same l)down m)up n)down o)same

Exercise 6-3
a)slight b) sharp c) dramatic d) steady

Exercise 6-4
a) sharply b)steadily c)slightly d) dramatically

Exercise 6-5
a)e b)e c)a d)e e)a f)a g)e h)e i)a j)a k)a l)a m)e n)e o)e

Exercise 6-7
1.f 2.b 3.j 4.k 5.d 6.e 7.m 8.h 9.d 10.j 11.l 12.a 13.i 14.l 15.e 16.e 17.k 18.g 19.i 20.l 21.j 22.k 23.c

Exercise 7-1
1. slide projector 2. screen 3. table (with figures) 4. graph 5. overhead projector (OHP) 6. pie chart 7. video 8. microphone 9. flipchart 10. bar chart 11. podium 12. sales folder 13. transparencies 14. remote control 15. pointer 16. marker/felt pen 17. notes 18. hand out

Exercise 7-2
Please, read the transcript

Exercise 7-3
1.b 2.c 3.d 4.b 5.c 6.c 7.a

ANSWER KEY

Exercise 7-4
1. interested 2. sensitive 3. living 4. economics 5. lend 6. rise 7. recipe 8. tell 9. delayed 10. remind 11. advice 12. conform 13. confidential 14. conscientious 15. price 16. to me 17. for 18. than

Exercise 7-5
1. inefficient 2. boring 3. uneconomical 4. unreliable 5. failed 6. agreed 7. impossible 8. made 9. permanent 10. irresponsible

Exercise 8-1
Otto Huber tel. 0041-25-6408/Urgent. Needs to speak with Mr. Wadsworth/Have him phone the Yodel Inn asap./Jannie/Amsterdam office/James staying another day. Have Ms. McCloud forward/his messages there./Pierre Duclot/Paris office/Have James Thorne return call asap. Good news.

Exercise 8-2
1. speaking 2. Hold the line please 3. I'm afraid he's rather tied up 4. Would you like to leave a message? 5. ask him to call me back 6. Really? 7. Could you say that slowly,

Exercise 8-3
a.5 b.3 c.6 d.2 e.1 f.4

Exercise 8-4
1. back 2. sorry 3. message 4. moment 5. busy 6. speaking 7. holiday 8. can 9. calling 10. tied up 11. details 12. hold 13. extension

Exercise 8-5
1.e 2.b 3.g 4.a 5.c 6.h 7.c 8.e 9.d 10.f 11.h 12.e

Exercise 8-6
Puzzle solution: GREAT

TRANSCRIPT

EXERCISE 1-2 IN THE CAR

José:
It seems strange to drive on the left-hand side of the road. I feel like I should be driving!

James:
Yes, I have the same feeling on the continent. But it's nice to see you again. Is this your first time in London?

José:
Yes, it is. I'd love to see some of the sights!

James:
Would you like me to show you around after the meeting?

José:
Would you? That's very nice of you. Is there a good tennis court near the hotel?

James:
Yes, there is. Are you interested in sports?

José:
Yes, a little to stay in shape. I play tennis and I enjoy swimming very much. What about you?

James:
I like tennis, too and I go skiing once a year. When I have time I go swimming or play squash.

EXERCISE 1-4 IN THE RESTAURANT

Head waiter:
Please show Mr. Thorne and his party to their table.

Waiter:
This way please. Here is your table Mr. Thorne. The wine list and menu, Sir.

James:
Thank you. But today we're celebrating. A bottle of your best champagne please.

The waiter brings a bottle of bubbly in a bucket of ice and pours a glass for everyone at the table.

TRANSCRIPT

James:
Mr. Wadsworth wasn't able to join us, but I know he would propose a toast to the success of Sun Club and our Virgin Islands project. So, here's to us. Cheers!

Everyone:
Cheers!

Jannie:
I'm so hungry. What do you recommend Penny?

Penny:
Roast beef and Yorkshire pudding is a traditional British speciality. It's very tasty.

Adriana:
Pudding with roast beef?

Penny:
It isn't really a pudding as the name suggests. It's a type of baked flour and egg dough. It's delicious.

Waiter:
Is everyone ready to order?

James:
Yes, I think so. Ladies first, of course.

Penny:
I'll have the cock-a-leekie as a starter and the Dover sole. I'd prefer a salad instead of vegetables, please.

Waiter:
We have a salad bar. You can help yourself to whatever you wish.

Jannie:
I'll try the roast beef.

Waiter:
Would you like it rare, medium or well done?

Jannie:
Medium, please. And instead of potatoes could I have rice?

Waiter:
Certainly.

TRANSCRIPT

Adriana:
I'll take the partan bree as a starter and the roast beef as well, but well done, please.

James gestures to José, Pierre and Fritz.

José:
I don't want a starter. Is the sole fresh?

Waiter:
Of course, Sir. It's served with fresh seasonal vegetables, sautéd in butter.

José:
Fine, then I'll try it. But I prefer rice rather than boiled potatoes.

Pierre:
I'll have the sole as well, but with potatoes, please.

Fritz:
I don't have lamb often, so I'll try the Welsh lamb. With vegetables and a salad, please.

Waiter:
Very well. Would you like to order a sweet now, or later?

James:
Later, I think.

Jannie:
James, I really have to try the chocolate cake. I love chocolate.

James:
Me too. OK. Anyone else?

Everyone else shakes their head no, except Adriana who would like strawberries and cream.

Fritz:
José, I'm going to Spain this summer on holiday. Will you be on holiday in August or at home?

José:
I'm not sure. Perhaps I'll just stay home or maybe we'll visit my girlfriend's family in America.

Pierre:
Oh, where is she from? I have friends in California.

José:
New York. But we'd like to just rent a car and drive where our hearts desire.

Adriana:
We want to visit some cousins in Australia this summer which, of course, means it's winter there. What about you Jannie?

Jannie:
My husband is American, so we're going to visit his relatives this summer in Florida and Massachusetts.

The waiter arrives with the food.

Waiter:
Enjoy your meal. Bon appetit.

EXERCISE 2-1 FORE !

Bill:
Playing some golf this weekend is a great idea. I really need the Exercise after that long flight.

James:
Actually, we're very lucky with the weather today. We don't get the chance to play very often.

Bill:
Well, neither do I. To tell you the truth, I haven't played in quite awhile, so I might be a bit rusty.

James:
Then let's go down to the driving range and hit a few balls first. Jonathan is already there. Afterwards we can spend some time on the putting green. We won't be teeing off until ten o'clock anyway.

Bill:
Fine. I'd like to get a feel for these clubs before I start playing.

James:
The pro shop looked well-stocked. I think you rented a nice set of clubs.

Bill:
Yeah, they look like new and I need all the help I can get. I really have to

work on my handicap. Perhaps one of the golf pros can give me a lesson before we play. The fairways look very challenging from here.

James:
It's an 18-hole championship golf course and the greens are very well-tended. I think you'll enjoy it, regardless of how well you do today.

Bill:
Just once I'd like to play several holes under par. That would give me a real sense of achievement.

James:
I know. Being a successful businessman isn't enough, is it?

Bill:
That's right, but I guess I'll have plenty of time to improve my golf game once I retire.

EXERCISE 2-5 CULTURAL AWARENESS

Penny:
Working for Sun Club has taught me a lot about arranging international meetings. You've also been a big help to me James. You always have something up your sleeve.

James:
It's not magic Penny. Remember, I was exposed at an early age to a variety of cultures. Little things have to be taken into account, such as the timing of meals, the selection of food, the names and titles used to address people with, whether an interpreter is necessary, getting materials through customs and allowing visitors who have traveled a long distance time to rest.

Penny:
Yes, it's important to cater to special cultural needs.

James:
My father would tell me interesting things he heard from the cultural attaché. An American golf ball manufacturer tried to sell golf balls in Japan. They were packed in boxes of four as usual, but didn't sell well. It seems the word for four in Japanese sounds much like the word for death.

Penny:
Selling products in another country can be frustrating. A friend in an advertising company told me about an ad he created in order to sell detergent in the Middle East. They showed the dirty clothes on the left, the soap in the middle

and the clean clothes on the right. Unfortunately, they forgot that people there read from right to left.

James:
That's like handing a business card to a Chinese with one hand.

Penny:
What's wrong with that?

James:
It's an offence, because according to Confucianism, the only way to present something is by using both hands.

Penny:
That reminds me of a silly one. An airline company that called itself after the Australian Emu. The bird can't fly.

James (laughing with Penny)
The most expensive mistake I've ever heard about though, involved a businessman who admired a sculpture he saw in the office of a Saudi Arabian businessman.
The Saudi was obliged by custom to give it to him. What the other man didn't know however, was that he had to give him a gift of equal value in return. The sculpture was worth $300,000.

Penny:
Wow! That must have been really embarrassing. And expensive, too!

James:
Yes, it was. Thank goodness, we only face minor differences most of the time. The Americans, for example, find it difficult to shake hands every morning when meeting, because it seems too formal. But it's very common in many European countries.

Penny:
On the other hand, the Europeans often complain when social activities are not scheduled for them when they're on business trips in the US.

James:
Yes. When it comes to international meetings we have to keep in mind that they can be very expensive and some mistakes can be very costly.

Penny:
I have my mini-checklist and notes from previous meetings to help me. But it isn't easy.

James:
You always come through, Penny! What would I do without you?

TRANSCRIPT

EXERCISE 3-1 AT THE CHECK-IN COUNTER

Agent:
Good morning sir. May I see your ticket please?

James:
Yes, I'm booked on the flight to Madrid which was cancelled.

Agent:
The flight has been cancelled due to safety reasons, but there is the possiblility of a transfer to flight No. 8153 to Paris. An immediate connection will be provided from there to Madrid.

James:
I have an important meeting scheduled this morning in Madrid. When will this flight arrive?

Agent:
You'll arrive approximately one hour later than the normally scheduled flight. We apologize for any inconvenience this may cause you and would be happy to inform any parties waiting for you that you will be unavoidably delayed.

James:
Well, it can't be helped. Yes, thank you. I would like a message sent.

Agent:
Please fill in this form. Would you put your luggage on the scales, please?

James:
I only have hand luggage.

Agent:
Fine. Where would you like to sit? Smoking or non-smoking?

James:
Non-smoking, please and on the aisle.

Agent:
I see you have a business class ticket. I'm terribly sorry Mr. Thorne, but we have only economy seats available for the transfer flight. We'll be happy to refund you the difference, plus compensation for the inconvenience.

James:
The flight is short enough. I'll live.

Agent:
Here's your boarding card, Mr. Thorne. Row 23 seat C.

TRANSCRIPT

James:

When do I have to be at the gate?

Agent:

You should be at the gate by 9:15. Have a nice flight and again, our sincerest apologies, Mr. Thorne.

James:

Thank you for your help.

EXERCISE 5-3 WHAT IS TQM?

Well, the first step was to get an external consultant to set up a two-day TQM workshop. He introduced the concept to the managers of the various departments in our hotel and gave everyone a better idea of what TQM means. First, we substituted what TQM stands for, with the new term, Total Quality Movement. We used the term "movement" to help us realize TQM is not something that can simply be imposed on a company's staff from the top, but rather a whole movement that has to work its way through to the roots of a company; right down to the bellboy and the cook's assistant. TQM means the whole company must think and act with quality in mind.

After the introductory workshop, the managers organized a workshop to explain the concept and its goals to his or her own staff. TQM is composed of several elements, two of which I'd like to tell you about in more detail. Firstly, the "customer-supplier relationship", and secondly, the "1-10 100 rule".

You may think the customer-supplier relationship is very clear in a hotel. We are the supplier and the customer is the guest. But TQM goes deeper than that. In order to deliver a better quality product, we had to learn that there are an endless number of customer-supplier relationships between the working staff of the hotel itself.

For example: A guest orders something at the dinner table. The waiter takes the order and relays it to the cook. In this case, the waiter is the supplier and the cook is the customer. Both have to agree on the product; namely, the contents of the order. As soon as the cook has done his job, he becomes the supplier and the waiter becomes the customer. Again, both have to be in agreement about the product and its standard of quality, so that the waiter can then pass the product on to the customer.

During each of these processes, of which there are many in the hotel business, each staff member is a supplier at one time and customer at another. TQM requires everyone involved to be aware of this relationship and to always be in agreement about the quality and content of the product to be delivered.

We also had to look at the definition of the word "quality". Quality doesn't mean a product has to be particularly fancy or expensive. Quality means "suitability for the purpose intended". When eating "fast-food", the quality of a hamburger is just as suitable as a tender filet steak is for enjoying a gourmet meal. The quality of the product is the same in both cases. The only difference is in its suitablility for the intended purpose.

If something is wrong with the product, the 1-10-100 rule applies. This rule simply says: the earlier a mistake is detected in the chain of processes, the lower the cost will be to correct it. Let me give you an example. A guest orders a pork chop with french fries. The waiter takes the order and relays it to the cook. The cook supplies a pork chop with boiled potatoes. If the waiter notices the mistake while he's still in the kitchen, the simple exchange of fries for potatoes costs very little time and effort. If, on the other hand, the mistake is not discovered until the meal has been served and the guest has complained, it's costlier to correct the mistake and the quality of the product has gone down.

The more complex a process is, the costlier correcting a mistake will be, the later it is discovered. Then it may not take one or ten man hours of time to correct, but 100 more man hours than it would have cost if the flaw had been detected right at the beginning.

We introduced TQM in our hotel half a year ago. Summarizing what we've accomplished, I can say today, that we're a lot more conscious of what actually takes place in our business. We talk more about the products we deliver to one another and we discuss their purpose, which is what quality is all about. And we are definitely more aware of how important it is to recognize a mistake at the beginning of a process. All this has surely contributed to the success of our hotel in the past six months.

TRANSCRIPT

EXERCISE 6-1

A. This form of communication should influence our target group's imagination in such a way, that, given a choice, a customer will choose our product. Using the many forms of media available, our main objectives will be: to establish a market share, to point out the positive characteristics of our product and to create a need for it in the minds of our potential customers.

B. It may be the most expensive marketing tool we use, but it is also the most effective. Through human contact and direct feedback we can personally advise and influence the most important members of our market and create a lasting bond.

C. This marketing instrument informs the public about the company, its aim, its position and its importance in the market. We use a conscious, systematic approach, based on public reaction, to build up confidence and good will in our enterprise, so that it will remain credible and transparent to our employees as well as our customers.

D. And last but not least, all actions of our sales team are supported and motivated by using this marketing method. Through a mailing action, a trade fair or a special event organized for our target group, we not only create new potential, but tie existing customers to our company as well. Using this instrument effectively can be the finishing touch of our advertising campaign.

EXERCISE 6-6

Same as text shown, see page 140

EXERCISE 7-2

First of all, don't get tense about being tense! Accept the fact that you're going to feel the same way most people do when they give a presentation: a little nervous. Tension can work for you. By moving your body naturally and gesturing with your hands, you can turn tension into energy and put life into your presentation.

To get rid of that funny feeling in your stomach before walking onto a stage, you can try a simple isometric exercise. Just tense your muscles, relax them and tense them again. Do this five times and you'll begin to feel your body relaxing. You can also breathe in slowly through your nose, hold your breath and then breathe out, counting to seven during each phase. You'll feel better almost immediately.

Secondly, start off with a good opening. You can use an interesting statistic, an amazing fact or a provocative question. An anecdote that refers to the needs and interests of your audience or a well-told joke are also effective. Whichever way you begin, make sure your opener runs smoothly by practising. During the first 30 seconds of your presentation, you have the chance to establish yourself and your message.

Thirdly, remember your eye contact with the audience. Look at your listeners and then speak. You can divide the room into sections and speak to a friendly face in each area. This way, you can systematically develop sympathetic listeners. Try to read faces and your audience's reaction. This will give you a chance to adapt your presentation, if you notice their attention is drifting.

Fourthly, if you're using visual aids, keep them simple. Have only one concept per slide or page and make sure your audience can get the point you wish to make at a glance. You're using visual aids to illustrate what you're saying, so don't read them and don't talk to them. Talk to your audience.

Fifthly, in dealing with a question, listen first. Don't try to think of an answer until you have understood the entire question. Keep your answer short and afterwards, re-establish eye contact with the rest of your audience. You can use eye contact to encourage people with friendly questions and avoid eye contact with those who might ask a question you choose not to answer. If you need a few seconds to organize an answer, you can use an opener like "If I understand you correctly, your question is ... / what you are asking is ..." or simply "That's a good question." If you can't answer a question, admit it. Saying "I'll find out the answer and get back to you." will gain you empathy and make you believable.

And lastly, rehearse again and again! I can't emphasize this enough. But should something go wrong during your presentation, don't panic. Adopt the attitude: "I won't let this situation get me down. I can handle it!"

TRANSCRIPT

EXERCISE 8-1

Hello, you have reached Sun International. Our office hours are from Monday to Friday 9a.m to 6p.m. We're sorry no one is in right now, but if you leave a message we will call you back as soon as possible. After the tone, please leave your name, telephone number and the reason for calling Sun International. Thank you.

Hello, this is Otto Huber speaking, manager of the Virgin Islands Club. It's very urgent that I speak to Mr. Wadsworth as soon as possible. Please ask him to call me first thing in the morning. He can reach me at Yodel Inn in Switzerland, at tel.no. 0041-25-6408. Thank you. Goodbye.

Hello, this is Jannie van Vliet speaking. James Thorne will be staying in Amsterdam a day longer. Please have Penny McCloud forward his messages to my office. Thank you. Goodbye.

Hallo, this is Pierre Duclot. I would like James Thorne to return my call at his earliest convenience. I have good news regarding the presentation. Merci.

GRAMMAR REFERENCE

1. THE SIMPLE PRESENT

(I am, he is, we are)

Example	Use
James **is** a troubleshooter. He **works** for Sun International. I **prefer** white wine. We usually **read** the Times.	for things in general, habits, permanent situation, feelings, timetables, opinions, etc.

Cue words:
every day/once a week/twice a month/three times a year
(at the end of a sentence)
never/often/usually/seldom/sometimes/always
(after the subject)

Example	Use
I **don't agree** with you. He **doesn't like** shrimp. **Do** you **work** for ....? **Does** she **work** for ....?	Use **do** as a *helping verb* to make the **negative** or to ask **questions**.

JOKE
"Waiter, do you have frog´s legs?"
"No sir, I always walk this way."

2. PRESENT CONTINUOUS

(I am doing, he is doing, we are doing)

Example	Use
Penny **is talking** to James We **are expanding** our Clubs. I'**m working** during the summer. Mr. Garfield **is arriving** tomorrow. **Are** you **doing** anything this evening? We'**re flying** to London next week.	An action happening now A temporary situation For future plans or arrangements

Note: *Some verbs are used in the present in the simple form only. Here are some of them:*

want	love	see	believe	suppose	forget
prefer	hate	hear	realize	mean	remember
wish	like	notice	know	understand	seem
belong	mind	smell	think(in believe)	have/own (to possess)	

JOKE
*"Please be quiet Tom, your father **is reading**."*
"Gee, I learned how to do that years ago!"

3. THE SIMPLE PAST

(I was, he was, we were)

Example	Use
The meeting **started** at 9 a.m. Bill **played** golf with James and Jonathan.	An action finished in the past with no connection to the future

Regular verbs take the **-ed** ending.
Irregular verbs have their own special forms (*see list in Index*).

Penny **went** to get everyone something to drink.
Mr. Garfield **told** Penny to call him Bill.

Did is the past form of **do** as a *helping verb* to ask questions, to give short answers and to make negatives:
Did you go to Paradise Cove Hideaway last month?

    Yes, I **did**. **Did** you?
    No, I **didn't**.

Penny **didn't** join the gentlemen at golf.
When **did** Mr. Garfield arrive?

The past form of **to be** is: I-he-she-it   **was**   **wasn't**
                                          we-you-they   **were**   **weren't**

Here are some cue words for the simple past:

yesterday　　　*last* night/week/month/year
the other day　　*two* days/weeks/months/years *ago*
until 1952　　*in* 1924

JOKE
At a laundry: "Madam, why the complaint? This handkerchief is perfect."
"It **was** a sheet before I **sent** it to your laundry!"

4. THE PAST CONTINUOUS

(I was doing, he was doing, we were doing)

Example	Use
James **was having** breakfast at 7a.m. What **were** you **doing** yesterday?	An action going on in the past at a certain time
Penny **was getting** the coffee while the men **chatted** in the office.	Both past forms are used when something else happens in the middle of an action
Mr. Garfield **was looking** for potential investors when he **heard** from Sun Club.	

JOKE
A car **was driving** at 150mph on the motorway when it **was stopped** by the police. "Sorry, Officer, **was** I **driving** too fast?" "No, Sir ... you **were flying** too low."

5. THE PRESENT PERFECT

(I have been, he has been, we have been)

This is the most confusing form in English because it has several uses. Think of it as a bridge from the past to the present:

GRAFFITI
An adult is someone who **has stopped**
growing *up* but not *out*.

Some important cue words:

just   *since* (point of time)   *for* (time period)   *still*   *ever*

never   *yet*   *up to now*   *already*   *lately*   *recently*   *so far*

Example	Use
Sales **have increased** this year.	Giving new information
So far, we **have had** good results.	Events started in the past with results in the present
James **has** *just* **left** the office.	Events that are a short time ago
Have you *ever* **been** to Hong Kong?	Asking if something has happened yet
I**'ve** *never* **seen** the Virgin Islands.	An action that could still happen
Have you **eaten** dinner *yet*?	Or it is something expected to happen?
Have you **seen** a good film *lately*?	
I**'ve worked** at Sun Club *for* 14 years.	An action that is not finished
She **has lived** in London *since* 1982.	

The difference between **gone to** and **been to**:

Where **has** James **gone**? (He is *on his way* somewhere or *still there*.)
Where **has** James **been**? (He *was somewhere* but has now *come back*.)

6. PRESENT PERFECT CONTINUOUS

(I have been doing, he has been doing, we have been doing)

The **-ing** form is found in every tense. Here the difference between simple and continuous forms of present perfect lies in the emphasis. The simple form emphasizes the **results** :

What **have** you **done** today? (*the speaker wants to know **what** you have accomplished up to now.*)

The **-ing** form emphasizes the **length of time** and that the action is probably **still going on**:

What **have** you **been doing** today? (*you are probably **still** doing something*)
Penny **has finished** the report for the feasibility study. (It's done.)
Penny **has been working** on the feasibility study. (She's probably still working on it.)

7. PAST PERFECT

(I had been, he had been, we had been)

This form is used when we talk about an action that happened before another action in the past. Later actions are in the simple past:

James **had thought** about taking over the Virgin Islands Club before he **called** Penny.
When James **called** Penny she **had** already **gone** to bed.

There is also an **-ing** form in the past perfect:

How long **had** Penny **been waiting** for James to call?

JOKE
A business that **had been marketing** a new cure for aspirin advertised:
"**Nothing**" helps faster than aspirin.

GRAMMAR REFERENCE

8. THE FUTURE
(I will, I won't)

Example	Use

I'll have the fish today.
We'll have a bottle of champagne.
He'll try on the shirt.
I **won't** eat the dessert. I'm on a diet.

Instant decision, it is not planned

I'll get you something to drink.
Will you please call me back later?
I asked Tom, but he **won't** do it.

To offer to do something
Asking someone to do something
Agreeing or refusing to do something

With the cue words :

maybe   perhaps   I hope   I think   hopefully   probably   I expect

Do you *think* they'll win the cup this year?
I *hope* you'll get the job.

A future prediction, what we think will happen

Sign in a pub
Don't complain about the beer.
One day you'll be old and weak too.

THE FUTURE
(I'm going to, he's going to, we're going to)

Example	Use

I'm **going to** go to bed early tonight.
James is **going to** visit Pierre.

An intention, or a decision to do something

JOKE
"Doctor, I think I'm dying."
"Nonsense, that's the last thing you're **going to** do."

GRAMMAR REFERENCE

9. MODAL VERBS

These are special verbs that help or add extra meaning to a verb and have more than one use.

Verb	Example	Use
Can	James **can** speak several languages.	The ability to do something
	Can I use your telephone?	Asking permission
	Can you quote a price for us?	A request
	James **can't** stop eating chocolate.	An inability to do something
Could	**Could** I ask a favor?	A request
	Could I interrupt you for a minute?	Asking permission
	We **could** lay off some workers.	A suggestion
Able to	I **haven't been able to** reach you.	
	He **wasn't able to** persuade him to sell.	

Could is *more polite* than **can** when asking for something. **Able to** is used when you speak of something further in the past or when someone has managed to do something:

May	**May** I borrow some money?	Asking permission
Might	It **might** be possible to see him Friday.	A future possiblility

May is *more polite* than **can** or **could** when asking for something. **Allowed to** is used when speaking further in the past or when something is forbidden. *You are **not allowed to** smoke here.*

Must	Passengers **must** fasten their seat belts.	You have to do it; an obligation
	You **musn't** smoke in the bathroom.	It is prohibited, forbidden
Have to	James **has to** go to the bank.	Same as must, but softer
	James **has to** fly to Paris.	

GRAFFITI
Mother's advice to her daughter:
*Before you find a prince, you **have to** kiss a lot of frogs!*

Must can only be used in the present. All other tenses use *"have to"*.

Would	What **would** you like to drink?	Offer
	Would you like to come to my party?	Invitation
	What time **would** be best next week?	Suggestion
	Would you please repeat that?	Request
Should	We **should** hire a new sales manager.	A recommended action
	We **should** have a meeting once a week.	

JOKE
*What tables **should** you eat? Vegetables.*

10. CONDITIONALS

You can put the **if** clause at the beginning or at the end of a sentence. In the first conditional we talk about what will or won't happen if you do, or don't do something.

Example

If there's a seat in business class, I**'ll take** that.
We**'ll give** a 2% discount, *if* you pay in cash.
If I see him, I**'ll tell** him you called.

Sign in a bar
If you drink like a fish, please swim home. Don't drive your car.

In the second conditional we talk about something that is *unlikely* or an *imaginary situation*. The **past** tense is used in the *if clause* and either **would, could,** or **might** in the *main clause*.

Example

If you **lost** your credit card, what **would** you do?
If I **won** the lottery, I **could** invest the money on the stock market.
If we **bought** bulk quantities, we **might** get a larger discount.

GRAFFITI
Culture is what your butcher
would *have if he* ***were*** *a surgeon.*

In the third conditional we talk about events which *could have happened* or those that *did happen* and we want to say how it *could have been different,* ***if.***

If you **had bought** stock in ... you **would have lost** a lot of money.
The employees **would not have gone** on strike *if* they **had received** a pay rise.
If Tom **had been** more careful he **wouldn't have broken** his leg skiing.

GRAFFITI in a nudist camp
If God ***hadn't wanted*** *us to be naked, we* ***would have been born*** *with clothes.*

11. RELATIVE CLAUSES

Example	Use
Fritz was the first person **who** interviewed Otto Huber.	*Who* is for people
The room **which** they use for meetings is very large.	*Which* is for things
The bank teller **that** James saw in Spain was beautiful.	*That* is for both
We want to go on a holiday **where** the sun is shining.	*Where* is for place
The man **whom** José spoke to sounded very friendly.	Used in formal, written English
Jannie is the one **whose** husband is American.	Used for the possessive

These clauses tell us exactly *which* person or thing, or *what kind of* person or thing (**that**) we are talking about and do not use a comma. Sometimes, who, which, that or whom can be left out and the meaning stays the same:

>The bank teller James saw ...   The man José spoke to ...

When we want to give *'extra information'*, we use commas, and **who** or **which** *can not be left out:*

Mr. Garfield, **who** *owns a hotel in the Virgin Islands*, is interested in Sun Club's proposal.
The contract, **which** *was signed yesterday,* included a four-day week.

GRAFFITI
*A neurotic is a person **who** builds castles in the air.*
*A psychotic is the person **who** lives in it.*
*A psychiatrist is the one **who** collects the rent.*

12. PASSIVE

(it is done/it was done etc.)

Example	Use
Sun International **is divided** into several divisions.	to describe an action, or process
The company **was founded** in 1954.	without saying who or
The invoices **have been paid** in full.	what did it

In the **passive** voice, the emphasis is moved from *'who did it'* to *'what was done'*. When we want to mention **who** did it, we use *'by'*. The **passive** is often used in English when it is understood **who** did the action or we are more interested in *the person or thing affected, rather than* **who** *did it.*

The **passive** is formed with *'to be'* as a helping verb, **plus** the past participle (third form for irregular verbs, **-ed** ending for normal verbs). Look at the following examples:

Active: Penny **checks** every fax that comes in for Sun Club.
Passive: Every fax **is checked** by Penny.

Active: Mr. Wadsworth **opened** the first Sun Club in 19..
Passive: The first Sun Club **was opened** in 19..

Active: Penny **has read** the faxes that came during the night.
Passive: The faxes that came last night **have been read** (*by* ...).

Active: Sun Club **is starting** the renovation of Paradise Cove Hideaway next week.
Passive: The renovation **is being started** at Paradise Cove Hideaway next week.

Active: The maid **was cleaning** the room when James arrived at the hotel.
Passive: The room **was being cleaned** when James arrived at the hotel.

> **GRAFFITI**
> High heels **were invented** by a woman **who** no longer wanted to be kissed on her forehead.

SPELLING

Spelling in English can be a challenge, even for native speakers, and the differences between British and American spellings adds to the confusion. Over the centuries, the English language has been influenced by numerous invasions of the British Isles by other peoples, and later by invading or colonizing other countries themselves. It is this wonderful mixture of many different languages that seems to give no logical pattern to spelling or to pronunciation in English.

There **are** spelling rules to help in English, but the exceptions may make you wonder why we have any rules in the first place. A general guide is better than no guide at all. Here are some of the most helpful rules:

GRAMMAR REFERENCE

i before e except after c

when the sound is **ee**

achieve	believe	receipt	receive
piece	chief	perceive	ceiling

BUT, there are the following exceptions:

either	their	beige	seize	weird	eight
foreign	freight	height	neither	leisure	weight

drop the y and add i (or ie)
(if there is a consonant before the y)

carry + ed = carr**ied**　　happy + ly = happ**ily**　　baby + s = bab**ies**

BUT not before a vowel:　enjoy + ed = enjo**yed**　　boy + s = bo**ys**
AND not before -ing:　carry + ing = carr**ying**　　hurry + ing = hurr**ying**

When a word ends in ie, change the ie to y before adding -ing:

lic + ing = l**ying**

Drop one l when adding full to a word

care + full = care**ful**　　thought + full = thought**ful**
Note: Full + fill = **fulfil**, UK

BUT *fully* is always with two *ll*'s : care**fully**　　thought**fully**

Double the l if there is one vowel in front of it:

signal + ed = signa**lled**　　dial + ed = dia**lled**

BUT not if there are two vowels in front of it:
feel + ing = feeling   fail + ed = failed

Double the last consonant of a one syllable word with only one vowel before an ending beginning with a vowel:

hot + er = ho**tt**er   swim + ing = swi**mm**ing   commit + ee = commi**tt**ee

BUT not when there are two vowels, two consonants or the word ends in a vowel:
cool + er = cooler   keep + ing = keeping   love + er = lover

With words of more than two syllables, it depends on the stress. The rule is then:

If the stress is on the final syllable, then the consonant is doubled.
If the final syllable is not stressed, then the consonant is not doubled.

recur + ing = recu**rr**ing   regret + ing = regre**tt**ing   begin + er = begi**nn**er
answer + ed = answered   offer + ing = offering

The art of spelling

APPENDIX

AMERICAN ENGLISH - BRITISH ENGLISH

US	UK	BRD
911	999	Notruf
answering machine	answerphone	Anrufbeantworter
apartment	flat	Wohnung
attorney, lawyer (trial lawyer)	solicitor, lawyer (barrister)	Rechtsanwalt
in the back	in the rear	hinten
ballpoint pen	biro	Kuli
bar	pub or bar	Kneipe
bill (dollar)	banknote (pound)	Schein
call (up)	ring (up)	anrufen
call collect	reverse charges	R-Gespräch führen
can	tin	Konservendose
candy	sweets	Süßigkeiten
car hood	bonnet	Motorhaube
car trunk	boot	Kofferraum
check/bill (restaurant)	bill	Rechnung
chips	crisps	Kartoffelchips
closet (built-in, eingebaut)	wardrobe	Kleiderschrank
coffee with cream	white coffee	Kaffee mit Milch
cookie	biscuit	Keks
desk clerk	receptionist	Rezeptionist
diaper	nappy	Windel
do/wash the dishes	do the washing up/wash up	Geshirr spülen
damn	bloody s. th.	verdammt
doctor's office	doctor's surgery	Arztpraxis
downsizing	rationalisation	Rationalisierung
downtown	town centre	Innenstadt
driver's license	driving licence	Führerschein
druggist	chemist	Apotheker
drugstore/pharmacy	chemist's/pharmacy	Apotheke
electrical outlet/ plug	power point	Steckdose
elevator	lift	Fahrstuhl
emergency ward	casualty department	Unfallstation/Notaufnahme
eraser	rubber	Radiergummi
exclamation point	exclamation mark	Ausrufezeichen
exit	way out	Ausgang
fall	autumn	Herbst

US	UK	BRD
faucet	tap	Wasserhahn
first floor	ground floor	Erdgeschoß
french fries	chips	Pommes Frites
front desk	reception	Rezeption
garbage/trash can	dustbin	Mülltonne
gas station	petrol station	Tankstelle
gas, gasoline	petrol	Benzin
get sick	be taken ill	krank werden
ground meat	minced meat	Hackfleisch
hold on	hold the line or hold on	am Apparat bleiben
in the hospital	in hospital	im Krankenhaus
to the hospital	to hospital	ins Krankenhaus
intersection	junction / crossroads	Abzweigung / Kreuzung
inventory	stock	Waren(Lager)stand
janitor	caretaker	Hausmeister
jumper cables	jumper leads	Überbrückungskabel
last name/family name	surname	Familienname
license plate	number plate	Nummernschild
line is busy	line is engaged	Leitung ist besetzt
liquor	spirits	alkoholische Getränke
long-distance call	trunk call	Ferngespräch
lost and found	lost property	Fundbüro
ma'am	madam	"gnädige Frau"
mail/mailbox	post/postbox	Post / Briefkasten
mailman	postman	Briefträger
make fun of/tease/ pull someone's leg	take the mickey out of/ having someone on	sich lustig über jdm. machen
mom/mommy	mum/mummy	Mutti
month.day.year	day.month.year	Reihenfolge bei Datum
motorcycle	motorbike or motorcycle	Motorrad
movie theater/movies	cinema/pictures	Kino
on Main Street	on the High Street	in der Hauptstraße
one-way ticket	single ticket	einfache Fahrkarte
nervous	nervy/nervous	nervös
pants	trousers	Hose
pantyhose	tights	Strumpfhose
parking lot	car park	Parkplatz
pen pal	penfriend	Brieffreund/in
period	full stop	Punkt (am Satzende)

US	UK	BRD
pie	flan	Torte
police officer/cop	PC, police officer/constable	Polizist
potato chips	crisps	Kartoffelchips
private school	public school	Privatschule
public school	state school	Staatliche Schule
purse/pocketbook/handbag	handbag	Handtasche
rent	let	vermieten
rent a car	hire a car	Auto mieten
restroom/john (coll.)	toilet/loo (coll.)	Toilette/Klo(coll.)
résumé	CV(curriculum vitae)	Lebenslauf
give someone a ride	give someone a lift	jdm. im Auto mitnehme
round-trip ticket	return ticket	Rückfahrkarte
rubber, condom	johnnie, French letter, condom	Kondom
have a seat	take a seat	nehmen Sie Platz
second floor	first floor	erste Etage
shot/injection	injection/jab	Spritze
sidewalk	pavement	Gehweg
smart	clever	klug
stand in line	queue	Schlange stehen
stingy, tight	mean, tight	geizig
stenographer	shorthand typist	Stenograph(in)
store	shop	Laden
stove	cooker	Herd
student	pupil or student	Schüler
subway	underground/in London tube	U-Bahn
sweater/pullover	sweater/jumper/pullover	Pullover
taxi stand	taxi rank or stand	Taxistand
telephone booth	phone kiosk/phone box	Telefonzelle
tennis shoes (sneakers, coll.)	trainers or tennis shoes	Sportschuhe
truck	lorry or truck	Lkw
TV	telly or TV	Glotzkiste
two weeks	fortnight	14 Tage
underpass (pedestrian)	subway	Unterführung
undershirt	vest	Unterhemd
undershorts/underwear	pants	Unterhose
at the university	at university	an der Uni
vacation (*but* public holiday)	holiday (*but* bank holiday)	Urlaub (*aber* Feiertag)
vacuum cleaner	Hoover or vacuum cleaner	Staubsauger
vest	waistcoat	Weste

APPENDIX

US	UK	BRD
on the weekend	at the weekend	am Wochenende
windshield	windscreen	Windschutzscheibe
yard	garden	Garten beim Haus
yield	give way	Vorfahrt gewähren
zip code	postal code	Postleitzahl

APPENDIX

INTERNATIONAL AIRLINE ALPHABET   BRITISH TELECOM

A- Alpha ä- Alpha echo	**A**- Andrew
B- Bravo	**B**- Benjamin
C- Charlie	**C**- Charlie
D- Delta	**D**- David
E- Echo	**E**- Edward
F- Foxtrot	**F**- Frederick
G- Golf	**G**- George
H- Hotel	**H**- Harry
I- India	**I**- Isaac
J- Juliet	**J**- Jack
K- Kilo	**K**- King
L- Lima	**L**- Lucy
M- Mike	**M**- Mary
N- November	**N**- Nelly
O- Oscar ö- Oscar echo	**O**- Oliver
P- Papa	**P**- Peter
Q- Quebec	**Q**- Queen
R- Romeo	**R**- Robert
S- Sierra sch- Sierra Charlie Hotel	**S**- Sugar
T- Tango	**T**- Tommy
U- Uniform ü- Uniform echo	**U**- Uncle
V- Victor	**V**- Victory
W- Whiskey	**W**- William
X- X-ray	**X**- X-Mas
Y- Yankee	**Y**- Yellow
Z- Zulu	**Z**- Zebra

Telex Abbreviations

Abbreviation	Meaning
A/C	account
ABT	about
ACC/ACCOM	accommodation
ADD	addition/additional
ADV	advise
AGN	again
APPROX	approximately
ARR/ARRNG	arrange/arrangement/arranging
ARV	arrive
ASAP	as soon as possible
ATTN	attention
CFM(D)	confirm(ed)
CHNG	change
CLD U	could you
CONTD	continued
DEL	deliver/delivery
DEP	departure
DISCT	discount
DLY	delay
DOC(S)	document(s)
DTD	dated
ETA	estimated time of arrival
FAO	for the attention of
FLGT	flight
FWD	forward
FYI	for your information
IFM	inform
INCL	including
INFO	information
INV	invoice
L/C	Letter of Credit
LST	last
LTR	letter
MAX	maximum
MIN	minimum

APPENDIX

MTG	meeting
+	and
NO	number
NXT	next
O/C	order confirmation
OK	I agree/ agreement
PLS	please
POSS	possible
RE/REF	about/reference
REC	received
RFI	request for information
RGDS	regards
RGRT	regret
RPLY	reply
RPT	repeat
SHPT	shipment
SRY	sorry
THKS	thanks
U	you
VST	visit
WK	week
WLD U	would you
YR	your

GR82CU

YYUR, YYUB
ICUR, YY4me

("Great to see you." "Too wise you are, too wise you be, I see you are too wise for me.")

INTERNATIONAL ETIQUETTE

Being successful in international business is not just dependent upon a good command of English or proficient negotiating skills. How you behave and what impression you make as a person can have just as strong an impact on the closing of a deal or in maintaining a good business relationship.

Knowing how to behave is fairly easy when dealing with your own countrymen. On an international level however, it can be a whole new ballgame. The French expression "Faux pas" meaning "indiscreet action, remark, etc., which offends against social convention", is just as commonly used and understood in English.

To keep you from "putting your foot into your mouth", or doing something equally inappropriate, here is an international hitlist of faux pas to avoid worldwide. Remember, you'll never get a second chance to make a good first impression.

APPENDIX
Faux pas Worldwide

NORTH AMERICA

Canada: lumping Canadians together with US-Americans; beginning a discussion about the language issue, economic problems or the separatist tendencies, particularly in Quebec.

USA: using surnames when addressing business friends; ignoring no-smoking signs or any other prohibitory signs; not owning a credit card; searching for a table on your own in a restaurant; blowing your nose during a meal; meager tipping; exaggerated use of polite phrases; beginning a discussion about religion, patriotism, domestic politics or scandals; referring to blacks as negroes instead of as African-americans.
Women: wearing pants to a business appointment; not wearing nylons; going topless (ditto for Canada).

SOUTH AMERICA

Impatience; punctuality; wearing casual clothes to a business appointment; bringing your wife to a business dinner; forgetting to bring a gift; leaving food on your plate; criticizing bullfighting; discussions about politics and religion.

EUROPE

Austria: conversations about politics and religion; beginning discussions about uncomfortable subjects such as Austria's entanglement in the National Socialist period, its treatment of foreigners and the tensions between Vienna and the individual states; forgetting to use academic titles.

The Baltic States: showing off with material goods; beginning conversations about the occupation between 1940-1991, and the suppressive measures of that period.

Belgium: discussions about the language issue; speaking French in Flanders or Flemish in Valais; wearing too conspicuous clothing; not having time for lunch.

Denmark: unpunctuality; bragging; discussions about World War II; negotiating business during lunchtime (11:30 a.m.-2.30 p.m.); visiting on business during July or August.

UK: criticizing conditions in Great Britain; not differentiating between English, Irish, Northern Irish, Scottish and Welsh; discussing business during dinner; making appointments before 9 a.m. or at the last minute; arriving too early; forgetting to use a title when addressing someone; touching personal things; speaking loudly; shaking hands except when being introduced or saying goodbye in a business situation; criticizing the weather; failing to show the proper respect when dealing with servants; lighting a cigarette before a toast has been given in honor of the queen.
Women: going topless.

Finland: neglecting the use of titles; unpunctuality; turning down an invitation, especially to a private sauna in someone's home; making jokes about Finnish alcohol consumption.

France: negligence in showing the proper respect for a meal; doing any serious negotiating before dessert; being too punctual; expressing any doubt about the importance of France in the world of fashion, literature and culture.

Italy: questions about domestic politics, corruption and the Mafia; comparing the affluent north with the economically poorer south when speaking to southern Italians, (Southern Italy begins south of Rome); neglecting the use of academic titles; forgetting to ask about the family; turning down an invitation; being unemotional; meager tipping.

The Netherlands: discussions about World War II; displaying know-it-all behavior; using academic titles.

Poland: beginning discussions about Polish-German, Polish-Russian or Polish-Jewish relations.

Sweden: unpunctuality; neglecting to take an oral agreement just as seriously as a written one; visiting on business during the summer vacation period; beginning a discussion about World War II.

Spain: criticizing bullfighting; making negative remarks about the church or its traditions; beginning conversations about regional tensions or acts of terrorism.

Switzerland: unpunctuality; acting like a know-it-all; discussions about World War II.

GUS: ignoring titles and rank; behaving or dressing in too brash or extroverted a manner; comparing technological developments in the West to those of Russia.
Women: wearing pants or too liberal clothing.

AFRICA

In general: making jokes about the host country; failing to respect African pride; referring to African blacks as negroes instead of Africans; beginning a discussion about African clans, tribes or communities; turning down an invitation to drink.

Egypt: failing to observe Egyptian hierarchy; impatience; trying to make business appointments before 10 a.m. and after 2 p.m. or on a Friday; using the left hand when presenting a gift; entering a mosque wearing shoes; beginning discussions about the Arab-Israeli conflict, Middle Eastern policies or the Third Reich.

MIDDLE EAST

Arabia: reaching out a hand to a woman on one's own initiative; handing something to someone with your left hand; refusing to try the local foods; crossing your legs and showing the soles of your shoes; asking for an alcoholic beverage; taking a picture without asking permission first.
Women: driving a car; dressing too liberally; taking part in official functions.

Gulf States: unpunctuality; discussing politics, especially Israel.

Israel: neglecting to segregate according to gender when using a group taxi; entering a synagogue without wearing a headcovering.

APPENDIX

Far East

In general: staying at a cheap hotel; forgetting to bring bilingual business cards; using your left hand when presenting your business card; demanding a knife and fork; talking about business during a meal.

Australia: unpunctuality.

China: criticizing the social system; impatience; speaking loudly; forgetting to use professional titles when addressing people; neglecting to respect hierarchy, rank and protocol; unpunctuality; presenting gifts before negotiations have begun; using blue and white giftwrapping paper; not bringing an appetite to a business meal; not reciprocating an invitation; making dirty jokes; tipping; using complicated arguments.

Hong Kong: doing anything that could cause your business partner to "lose face"; neglecting to exchange business cards; talking about failures; not reciprocating an invitation; wearing leisure or entirely white clothes.

Singapore: giving gifts to government officials; giving flowers, knives or alarm clocks as gifts; making compliments.

India: speaking to a woman alone in public; displaying hectic behavior; criticizing the culture; using the left hand; beginning discussions about sex, religion, the caste system, and the poor; praising Pakistan.

Indonesia: Western business dress or being overdressed; conversations about politics and religion; ordering pork as a host; unpunctuality.

Japan: failing to respect Japanese hierarchy and protocol; forgetting to bow; addressing someone using their first name; turning down an invitation to a nightclub; wearing shoes when entering a private home; looking a person in the eyes for too long; shaking hands; black or white giftwrapping paper; gaps in knowledge about your product; scribbling notes on business cards; forgetting to send New Year's greetings; behaving in too loud a manner.

Malaysia: giving gifts to government officials; pointing at someone; touching food with the left hand (Moslem tradition).

Philippines: criticizing the country and its strong Catholicism; praising the Chinese.

Thailand: addressing someone using their surname; touching someone's head, shoulder or back; touching someone with your foot; shaking hands; stepping on the threshold of a door; entering someone's home wearing shoes; discussions about the monarchy, the frequent military putsches or religion; eating with the left hand; displaying hectic behavior.

Do´s in Great Britain and in the United States

Now that you know some of the "don'ts" when meeting with international business partners, here are some "do's" that can make life easier for you in dealing with business associates from Great Britain and the United States.

Great Britain

Dress: Since Great Britain is still a fairly conservative country, a dark grey or blue suit is recommended when attending a business meeting. On festive occasions, such as a day at the horse races in Ascot or Epsom, very formal dress is appropriate: a morning suit with a grey top-hat for the gentlemen and a long gown or cocktail dress with a hat for the ladies.
Names: Using first names when addressing one another is common after a relatively short period of time. This does not mean you have become "best buddies". It is simply a less formal way of dealing with people.
Gifts: Don't be too cheap. An elegant writing utensil or an attractive keyring out of some valuable material is appropriate for a business partner, whereas an especially beautiful scarf is nice for the wife. When bringing alcohol, an especially fine wine from your country is recommended. A good bottle of real champagne is also acceptable.
Remember: Great Britain is comprised of four regions: England, Scotland, Wales and Northern Ireland. In referring to a particular region when discussing sports or business, consider the national identity and pride involved and differentiate.
Although class differences are diminishing, they are more readily observable in Great Britain than in other European countries. These differences can express themselves in the type of language used, former education, the school the children attend, dress and the area one lives in.

Displaying polite, friendly and tolerant behavior, regardless of whom you're dealing with, is appreciated by everyone.

THE UNITED STATES

Dress: Forget the picture of the typical American tourist. In business life Americans can be far from casual or informal in what they wear. Prestigious restaurants, hotels and offices will not receive guests without a tie.

Names: An American will be on a first-name-basis with a guest or partner very quickly. Wait until he makes the first step. As in Great Britain, don't expect this to mean you have an especially close relationship. Using first names just makes life easier in dealing with people.

Titles: In addressing someone verbally, academic titles are rarely used. It is considered bragging and rather undemocratic. The title "Dr." is primarily used when referring to a medical doctor or in academic circles when writing a letter. Exceptions to the rule of using first names are found when addressing the President of the United States or the Secretary of State. In this case, "Mr. President" or "Mr. Secretary" is appropriate. The use of "Sir" or first names is acceptable for other members of the government.

Punctuality: Is taken seriously and also expected of guests.

Invitations: Just as in most Northern European countries, an invitation is to be taken seriously when a concrete time and place have been agreed upon, but not necessarily when an invitation like "Come visit me anytime!" is mentioned in passing, á la small talk.

Guests: American guests don't expect much time to be spent on drinking and eating during business hours. However, an invitation to have a typical European meal is always popular.

The conception of time: In dealing with the world around him, no matter how busy an American is, he usually gives the impression he has time for you. In professional life, people make time for one another, despite a hectic schedule. Try to behave in a similar fashion when receiving American guests. Give a visitor the impression you have reserved a lot of time for him. (Displaying hectic behavior or demonstrating how busy you are, doesn't impress anyone in the States.)

Efficiency: For the American businessman, the crucial question is always: will an economic measure be beneficial or profitable in the long-run? This weighing of "cost versus benefits" rules American firms. Whoever is inefficient gets fired. Don't be surprised by this attitude and don't underestimate the power of the so-called "controller".

Hard bargaining: In closing a deal, expect friendly but tough bargaining. All important negotiations are accompanied by the presence of an attorney. Getting a tough, prestigious, experienced attorney to help in dealing with difficult negotiations is highly recommended.

Conversation: Good topics for conversation are always the environment, the stock market and American football.

Humor: Both the Americans and the British make an effort to loosen up a situation or reduce the stress and tension of business life with humorous remarks or comments. Remember: you too will be judged by your sense of humor. (Being cynical or making jokes at the expense of others is not considered funny.)

And last but not least, the golden rule is: when in doubt, ask. Everyone will understand if you, as a foreign guest, are unsure about something. After all, giving a person the chance to help you will make them feel good and you, as a person, appear all the more human.

(The authors and publisher would like to thank the ECON publishing group, Düsseldorf, for its kind permission in using some of the information on etiquette loosely compiled from the book "Der Neue Manager Knigge" by Heinz Commer, 1993)

beeing very polite

Sprachen lernen mit Superlearning

leicht, schnell, intensiv für Selbstlerner

Englisch für Import & Export

Speziell für die berufliche Anwendung ist der neue Kurs „English for Import & Export" konzipiert. Für alle, die etwas für ihren Erfolg „on the job" tun wollen und bereits über englische Vorkenntnisse verfügen, bietet dieser Kurs Redewendungen, technische Begriffe und Fachausdrücke aus dem Bereich Außenhandel. Sie lernen 1000 der wichtigsten Vokabeln und üben die Abwicklung folgender Geschäftsvorgänge in englischer Sprache:

- Briefe, Faxe und Telexe verfassen
- Angebote einholen und unterbreiten
- Zollformalitäten erledigen
- Telefonate führen
- Reklamationen bearbeiten

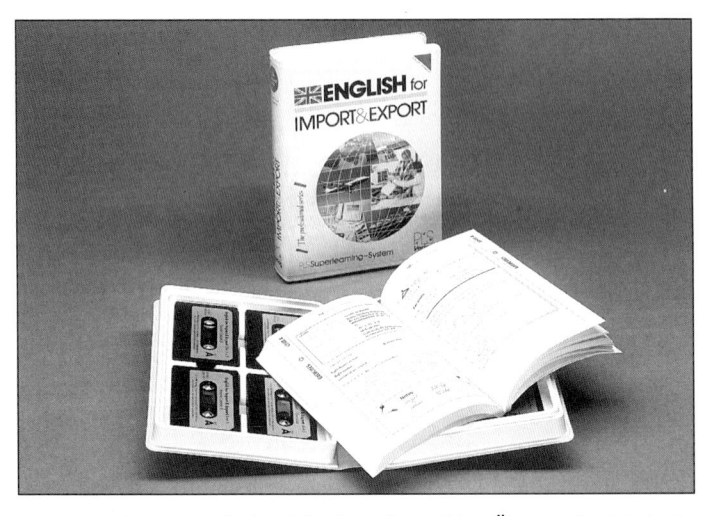

8 Kassetten (ca. 8 Stunden), Lehrbuch, umfangreicher Übungsteil, alphabetisches Vokabular, Fachglossar, Lernanleitung, Entspannungstraining.
Best.-Nr. 444-075-9
DM 198,– / öS 1545 / sFR 198,–

Bitte fordern Sie den Gesamtkatalog an

PLS Sprachen   JÜNGER VERLAG, Postfach 10 09 62
63069 Offenbach · Tel. 0 69 / 84 00 03–21 · Fax

GABAL Business-Bücher aus der Praxis für die Praxis

Beruf & Karriere

Josef W. Seifert
Visualisieren, Präsentieren, Moderieren
176 Seiten, A5, Illustrationen
DM 29,80/öS 233/sFR 29,80
ISBN 3-930799-00-6

Vera F. Birkenbihl
Stroh im Kopf?
Gebrauchsanleitung fürs Gehirn
- vom „Gehirn-Besitzer" zum
„Gehirn-Benutzer" 180 Seiten,
A5, viele Abbildungen
DM 29,80/öS 233/sFR 29,80
ISBN 3-923984-99-5

Alexander Groflmann
Erfolg hat Methode!
Durch ganzheitliches
Selbstmanagement effektiver
arbeiten, seine Zukunft gestalten, glücklicher leben
160 Seiten, A5, viele Abb.
DM 29,80/öS 233/sFR 29,80
ISBN 3-930799-03-0

Berthold Ulsamer
Exzellente Kommunikation mit NLP
Als Führungskraft den Draht zum anderen finden
152 Seiten, A5, viele Abb.
DM 29,80/öS 233/sFR 29,80
ISBN 3-923984-48-0

Lothar J. Seiwert
Das neue 1 x 1 des Zeitmanagement
Zeit im Griff, Ziele in Balance, Erfolg mit Methode
128 Seiten, A5, 4farbig, Abb.
DM 24,80/öS 194/sFR 24,80
ISBN 3-923984-89-8

Manfred Lucas
Hören - Hinhören - Zuhören
150 Seiten, A5
viele Abbildungen
DM 24,80/öS 194/sFR 24,80
ISBN 3-923984-98-7

Harald Scheerer
Reden müßte man können
Selbstbewußt auftreten,
Persönlichkeit einsetzen,
Zuhörer begeistern
136 Seiten, A5
viele Abbildungen
DM 24,80/öS 194/sFR 24,80
ISBN 3-923984-38-3

Lothar J. Seiwert
Selbstmanagement
Persönlicher Erfolg, Zielbewußtsein, Zukunftsgestaltung
80 Seiten, A5, viele Abb.
DM 24,80/öS 194/sFR 24,80
ISBN 3-923984-45-6

Winfried U. Graichen, Lothar J. Seiwert
Das ABC der Arbeitsfreude
Techniken, Tips und Tricks für Vielbeschäftigte
80 Seiten, A5, viele Abb.
DM 24,80/öS 194/sFR 24,80
ISBN 3-923984-43-X

Mogens Kirckhoff
Mind Mapping
Einführung in eine kreative
Arbeitsmethode
126 Seiten, A4, 4farbig
DM 36,00/öS 281/sFR 36,00
ISBN 3-923984-80-4

Für weitere Titel fordern Sie bitte unseren kostenlosen Gesamtkatalog an:
GABAL VERLAG / 63069 Offenbach, Postfach 10 09 62,
Tel. 0 69 / 84 00 03-21, Fax -33 oder in Ihrer Buchhandlung.

JÜNGER GABAL Audio-Selbstlernprogramme

Becker/Schenten
Sich selbst und andere bewegen
Mehr Leistung durch Bewegung
1 Tonkassette, Bewegungsbuch
mit Bewegungskarten
ISBN 3-89467-272-2
DM 79,- /öS 553/sFR 79,-

Rudolf Straube
Mehr Lebensfreude durch Streßbewältigung
Bewußt ein streßfreies und somit effektiveres Leben führen
2 Tonkassetten, Arbeitsbuch
ISBN 3-89467-286-2
DM 79,- /öS 553/sFR 79,-

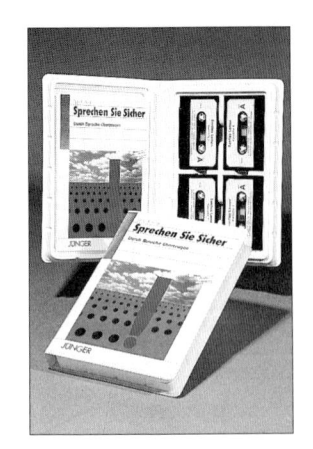

Peter R. Heigl
Sprechen Sie sicher
Rhetorikkurs um Gespräche, Reden und Vorträge sicher und ausdrucksvoll zu führen
4 Tonkassetten, Arbeitsbuch
ISBN 3-89467-127-0
DM 126,- /öS 882/sFR 126,-

Herbert Namokel
Die moderierte Besprechung
Arbeitstechniken und Methoden zur Steuerung und Führung von Besprechungen
1 Tonkassette, Arbeitsbuch
ISBN 3-89467-271-4
DM 59,- /öS 413/sFR 59,-

Winfried Erb
Konfliktfreie Gesprächsführung
Konflikte auf konstruktive Weise zu lösen.
1 Tonkassette, Arbeitsheft
ISBN 3-927225-13-4
DM 39,- /öS 273/sFR 39,-

Susanne Köster
Fähigkeiten erkennen, entfalten, nutzen
Lebensqualität + Erfolg
mit NLP
2 Tonkassetten, Arbeitsbuch
ISBN 3-89467-217-X
DM 79,- /öS 553/sFR 79,-

Für weitere Titel fordern Sie bitte kostenlos unseren Gesamtkatalog an:
JÜNGER VERLAG / **63069 Offenbach, Postfach 10 09 62**
Tel. 0 69 / 84 00 03-21, Fax -33 oder in Ihrer Buchhandlung.